AF600405

THE CATHOLIC UNIVERSITY OF AMERICA
CANON LAW STUDIES
Number 63

THE ACT OF RELIGIOUS PROFESSION

A BRIEF HISTORICAL SYNOPSIS AND COMMENTARY

A DISSERTATION

SUBMITTED TO THE FACULTY OF CANON LAW
OF THE CATHOLIC UNIVERSITY OF AMERICA
IN PARTIAL FULFILLMENT OF THE REQUIREMENTS
FOR THE DEGREE

DOCTOR OF CANON LAW

BY THE

REV. WOLFGANG N. FREY, O.S.B., A.B., J.C.L.
OF ST. VINCENT ARCHABBEY, LATROBE, PA.

THE CATHOLIC UNIVERSITY OF AMERICA
WASHINGTON, D.C.
1931

IMPRIMI PERMITTIMUS:

✠ALFREDUS KOCH, O.S.B., S.T.D.
Archiabbas S. Vincentii.

Archiabbatia S. Vincentii, die XIX Martii, A.D. 1931.

NIHIL OBSTAT:

VALENTINUS T. SCHAAF, O.F.M., J.C.D.
Censor Deputatus

IMPRIMATUR:

✠HUGO CAROLUS BOYLE, D.D.
Episcopus Pittsburgensis

Pittsburgi, die XX Martii, A.D. 1931.

COPYRIGHT, 1931
THE CATHOLIC UNIVERSITY OF AMERICA

TABLE OF CONTENTS

PRINCIPAL ABBREVIATIONS

AAS	—*Acta Apostolicæ Sedis.*
ASS	—*Acta Sanctæ Sedis.*
AER	—*American Ecclesiastical Review.*
AkKR	—*Archiv für Katholisches Kirchenrecht.*
Coll. Lac.	—*Acta et Decreta S. Conciliorum Recentiorum.*
CpR	—*Commentarium pro Religiosis.*
Fontes	—*Codicis Juris Canonici Fontes.*
HPR	—*Homiletic and Pastoral Review.*
IER	—*Irish Ecclesiastical Record.*
LQS	—*Theologisch-Praktische Quartalschrift.*
Mansi	—Mansi, *Sacrorum Conciliorum Nova et Amplissima Collectio.*
MPG	—Migne, *Patrologiæ Cursus Completus, Series Græca.*
MPL	—Migne, *Patrologiæ Cursus Completus, Series Latina.*
NRT	—*Nouvelle Revue Theologique.*
RCR	—*Revue des Communautes Religieuses.*

FOREWORD

THE primary idea of the religious state was proclaimed by our Divine Master, Jesus Christ, in those words which were recorded by St. Mathew, "If thou wilt be perfect, go sell what thou hast and give to the poor; and come follow me."[1]

The underlying principle, therefore, of this state of perfection is the renunciation of the world and its perishable possessions in order the better to live in close union with the Divine Master. St. Thomas of Aquin calls those religious who devote themselves entirely to the Most High, by offering themselves as a holocaust to Him.[2]

Entrance into the religious state is obtained by means of religious profession. Profession may be called the gateway to religious life. Everyone who passes through these portals takes upon himself the obligation of striving after Christian perfection in an especial manner, by faithfully making use of the means of perfection offered in the religious life. These means toward perfection are in particular the vows of religion: Chastity, poverty, and obedience. From a canonical point of view the entire superstructure of the religious obligation of the individual depends upon the validity of the profession. It is the purpose of this treatise to point out, and to explain the various requirements which the Code of Canon Law sets down for the validity of the act of profession.

In the First Part, the historical background of the present legislation is outlined. The history of religious profession during the early centuries of its existence is, in the main, the history of the customs of the early monastic communities surrounding the admission of aspirants to religious life. Sources for this early history will naturally be confined to the rules and customary regulations of the various monastic communities then in existence. In the course of the centuries, however, definite ecclesiastical legislation became necessary to preserve order and uniformity in the great monastic family. Consequently, as circumstances demanded, the Church, through the Pontiffs, the synods, and councils, issued numerous decrees and regulations on various

[1] *Matt.* XIX, 21.

[2] *2a, 2ae*, q. 186, art. 1.

points of religious profession. These legislative pronouncements of the Holy See may, in a general way, be grouped under two main headings, namely: the mode of making profession; and the nature of profession. Under the first heading legislation pertaining to express and tacit profession is treated, while the second grouping has to do with the distinction between solemn and simple profession; the origin and development of congregations of simple vows; and finally perpetuity of religious profession. The history of profession, as outlined in this treatise, is by no means presented as an exhaustive study. It is intended merely to give the high lights in the development of the present legislation on the subject.

The present law on religious profession is dealt with in the Second Part. The tract on religious profession forms the third chapter of title eleven in the second book of the Code, and embraces canons 572 to 586 inclusive. The tract on profession may be divided into two sections, namely, that treating of the *act* of profession, or the *professio in fieri*, and that treating of the *state* of profession, which may be called the *professio in facto esse*. The first part alone—the act of profession—that is the *professio in fieri*, is considered in the pages that follow. The canons which have bearing on the validity and the liceity of this act constitute the subject matter of the second part of this treatise. A preliminary chapter on the personal qualifications of aspirants to religious life has been inserted. Because so intimately connected with the act of profession, a short chapter has been added on the disposal of property which every religious must make before his profession. Profession of those who are obliged to military service, and the privilege of death-bed profession of novices are treated in two appendices. Although these two subjects find no place among the canons of the Code, they are nevertheless a part of the Church's legislation on profession, and therefore they must necessarily come up for discussion in the present treatise.

The author welcomes this opportunity to manifest his gratitude to his Superiors for the privilege of advanced studies; to his Confreres in religion for their interest and encouragement, and for their many acts of kindness. To the Faculty of the School of Canon Law he expresses his deep appreciation for their generous assistance and guidance in the preparation of this monograph.

PART I

HISTORICAL DEVELOPMENT

CHAPTER I

RELIGIOUS PROFESSION IN GENERAL

WHEN referred to religious life, the word *profession* is used to signify the act whereby a person publicly embraces the religious state.[1] Authors, in their writings concerning the subject of religious profession, give a variety of definitions. Reiffenstuel[2], and Makee[3], define profession as "a voluntary promise, lawfully accepted, by means of which a person, after having attained the prescribed age, and having spent the required year in probation, binds himself to an approved religious order." Augustine[4] describes it as "an external act of the mind by which one embraces the religious state, or the external testimony of one who aspires to be a servant of God." A more comprehensive definition is set down by Schmalzgrueber who defines religious profession as "the act of a person who, in virtue of the three vows of poverty, chastity, and obedience, freely gives himself to God in an approved order, through the intervention of a lawfully constituted superior accepting this surrender of self in the name of God and of the religious order."[5]

In a very broad sense profession is a public manifestation of the will, by which a person makes known his intention of striving after perfection in a particular state of life. Taken in this broad significance the making of vows is not essentially necessary to constitute a profession. It is in this broad interpretation of the term that members of Third Orders Secular may be said to

[1] Humphrey, *Elements of Religious Life*, p. 81.

[2] *Jus Canonicum Universum*, lib. III, tit. XXXI, n. 157.

[3] *Institutiones Juris Ecclesiastici*, I, 489.

[4] *Commentary*, III, 252.

[5] "Actus religiosus et sacer, per quem homo fidelis, in religione aliqua approbata, per emissionem trium votorum substantialium paupertatis, castitatis, et obedientiæ, voluntarie se Deo tradit, interveniente auctoritate prælati qui hujusmodi traditionem Dei et religionis nomine acceptet."—*Jus Ecclesiasticum Universum*, pars IV, tit. XXXI, n. 149.

make profession even though they take no vows. By becoming members of these societies they signify their determination of striving after perfection by observing the statutes of the society; they do not, however, bind themselves to this observance by any vows. But in its strict and proper signification, religious profession is more than a mere manifestation of intention or determination on the part of the religious, to strive after perfection—it is a juridical act, a contract entered into by the candidate for the religious institute on the one hand, and by the religious institute itself on the other.[1]

Three necessary elements must be present to form a religious profession, properly so called. These elements are vows, *traditio* or surrender of self, and acceptance by a competent superior.

Vows

A vow may be defined a "deliberate, voluntary promise made to God concerning some possible and better good."[2] A vow is a promise which induces an obligation in conscience. In this it differs from a simple resolution. The latter, no matter how seriously it may have been made, does not of its own power impose an obligation under pain of sin; it is true that a person making a resolution might, in some particular case, intend thus to bind himself. A vow, on the contrary, by its own power, imposes an obligation in conscience.

Vows are essential to every religious profession. In other words, no profession, properly so called, can exist without vows. In defining the religious state, the Code of Canon Law bears out this fact. In enumerating the necessary elements of the religious state, the Code says that it is a permanent mode of living in common by which the faithful observe the Evangelical Counsels of obedience, chastity and poverty by means of vows.[3] In order to show further the necessity of vows for religious profession,

---

[1] "...professio est contractus...bilateralis, in quo nempe contrahentium obligatio est reciproca vel mutua."—Vicente, *Recentia Instutita*, tract. II, cap. V, n. 194; "...est contractus inter religionem et professum,"—Sipos, *Enchiridion, J. C.*, p. 314; "Profession implies an agreement between the individual and the institute..."—Papi, *Religious in Church Law*, p. 268.

[2] Can. 1307, §1; Augustine, *Commentary*, VI, 289.

[3] Can. 487.

one need only to examine the significance of profession. By profession a person enters into the religious state and consecrates himself to God. The religious state, of its very nature, demands stability,[1] perseverance of its members in that state. This stability cannot be gained effectively from any obligation arising from an extrinsic authority; the necessary binding force must come from within; it must proceed from the will of the one who embraces this state. Such a binding force can arise only from a vow,[2] for, as Pruemmer says, this stability must be such that the religious would be guilty of sin against both the divine and the ecclesiastical law if he should presume to leave the religious state without the proper dispensation.[3]

The end and aim of the religious state is to provide for its members the means of attaining perfection, by removing the obstacles which hinder progress in perfection. This it does by prescribing that every one of its members make the vows of poverty, chastity, and obedience. Poverty, against the allurements of the world with its riches and comforts; chastity, against the flesh and its unruly passions and its desires for pleasure; and finally, obedience, to overcome self, ever proud, ever self-willed, ever striving to gain the mastery over others.[4]

These three vows, therefore, are necessary to the religious state, and in consequence must be one of the constituents of every religious profession.[5]

Surrender of Self

An individual in the world may bind himself by a vow to observe poverty, chastity, and obedience, and yet not make religious profession. By the profession the religious contracts a spiritual

---

[1] "Status religiosus" (est) "stabilis in communi vivendi modus..."—C. 487; "Status religiosus...requirit magnam immobilitatem cum objectivam tum subjectivam..."—Pruemmer, *Manuale*, *J. C.*, q. 170.

[2] Suarez, *De Statu Perfectionis et Religionis*, lib. II, cap. 3, n. 5.

[3] "Ista immobilitas conditionis oportet esse tanta ut homo (sine legitima dispensatione) deserendo talem statum libere electum, peccet contra legem cum divinam tum ecclesiasticam..."—*Manuale J. C.*, q. 170.

[4] St. Thomas, *2a, 2ae*, q. 186, a. 7.

[5] Cf. can. 487; Pruemmer, *Manuale J. C.*, q. 170; Papi, *Religious Profession*, p. 3.

tie which binds him to the religious institute[1]. A person, to become a religious must renounce all claims upon himself and must give his entire self, body and soul, to God in the religious order or congregation. Hence besides the vows every religious must include a surrender of self[2] to the religious community in which he intends to follow his vocation.[3]

Profession partakes of a two-fold character: it embraces a spiritual and a human character.[4] Its spiritual character consists in the voluntary promise made to God, in virtue of which the religious obliges himself to observe the Evangelical Counsels. But this he promises to do not in an indefinite, undetermined manner, but in accordance with the prescriptions and rules of a particular religious institute—and in this rests the human character of profession. In order to make possible the fulfillment of the human character, the candidate must give up his rights together with his own self, and cede these to the institute in which he intends to carry out his vows. It is precisely in this that the *traditio* or surrender of self consists. In virtue of this surrender the religious assumes the obligation of observing the rule and the statutes of the Community he enters. Hence from every profession there arises a double obligation for the religious: one toward God by reason of the vows; the other toward the religious community because of the surrender of self[5]. Therefore, that one become a religious it is not sufficient that he make only vows; it is absolutely necessary that together with the vows he surrender himself to the Institute.[6]

---

[1] Piontek, *De Indulto Exclaustrationis necnon Sæcularizationis*, p. 75.

[2] "This...surrendering of self to an institute is something distinct from the taking of vows, although both are accomplished by the same act."—Papi, *Religious Profession*, p. 4.

[3] "...ubi deest talis traditio, deest status religiosus, deest illa stabilitas et firmitas coram Ecclesia, quam visibile regimen requirit..."—Sipos, *Enchiridion J. C.*, p. 314.

[4] "Il y dans la profession religieuse un double engagement: l'un vis-à-vis de Dieu; l'autre vis-à-vis de l'Eglise..."—Mercier, "Les voeux solennels de Religion d'apres le Code," *Revue Thomiste*, 27 (1922), 401.

[5] Humphrey, *Elements of Religious Life*, p. 27; Papi, *Religious in Church Law*, p. 268.

[6] Pope Alexander II declared the profession of a certain priest, Consaldus null and void, because it lacked this essential quality.—C. 1, C. XVII, q. 2. Cf. also Suarez, *De Statu Perfectionis et Religionis*, lib. VI, cap. 2, n. 4.

Acceptance

On the part of the religious who makes profession, only the two elements (vows and surrender of self) are necessary; but in order that his profession have binding force, a third element is required: it must be accepted by a lawfully constituted superior.[1] Religious profession is a contract, of which the contracting parties are the candidate and the religious institute. The candidate binds himself to observe the monastic rule,[2] while the institute, on the other hand, assumes the obligation of providing for the temporal and spiritual needs of the religious.[3]

In order that any contract have binding force, a manifestation of consent of the contracting parties is required. Hence that the mutual obligation of religious profession have existence, the making of profession on the part of the religious will not suffice. It is necessary that the religious institute accept this profession of the candidate, which it does through its lawfully constituted superior.

---

[1] Can. 572, §1, 6°.

[2] Vicente, *Recentia Instituta*, tract. II, cap. V, n. 194.

[3] Papi, *Religious in Church Law*, p. 268.

CHAPTER II

EARLY HISTORY OF PROFESSION

ARTICLE 1

FROM ITS ORIGIN TO THE EARLY MONASTIC COMMUNITIES

Religious life may be traced back to the very early ages of the Christian era. Already in Apostolic times both men and women practiced the Evangelical Counsels of chastity, poverty, and obedience.[1] The Christian virgins were the first[2] to lead lives distinct from those of the remainder of the faithful. Striving after perfection in an eminent degree, they lived in perfect chastity, and in order to attach themselves even more closely to their Divine Spouse, Jesus Christ, many of them renounced their temporal possessions, following in this the voice of the Master: "If thou wilt be perfect, go sell what thou hast...and come follow me."[3] In the beginning these Virgins did not separate themselves from the general body of the faithful, but strove after a life of perfection in the midst of their own family circle.[4] But in the course of time they began to separate themselves from the remainder of the faithful, in order to carry out their noble design with greater ease and perfection.[5]

---

[1] Schaefer, *Das Ordensrecht*, p. 6; Turner, *The Vow of Poverty*, pp. 3–4; Besse, *Moines d'Orient*, p. 22.

[2] Vermeersch, "Religious Life," *Cath. Encycl.*, XII, 750; Smith, *Christian Monasticism*, p. 215.

[3] *Matt.*, XIX, 21.

[4] "The earliest Christian...finds no institution of asceticism with which he may ally himself, no group whom he may join in the pursuit of asceticism... Accordingly he enters upon a life of continence, surrounding himself with such safeguards as he deems fit..."—Murphy, *St. Basil and Monasticism*, p. 8; cf. also Heimbucher, *Die Orden und Kongregationen*, I, 58; Scharnagl, *Das Feierliche Gelübde als Ehehinderniss*, p. 16; Smith, *Christian Monasticism*, p. 215.

[5] "Dans la seconde moitié du IIIe siècle, on voit des ascètes se séparer des

Shortly after the Virgins began to consecrate themselves wholeheartedly to Christ in perfect chastity, men undertook to lead lives similar to those lived by the Virgins.[1] They, in the course of time, became known as the Ascetics. The name *Ascetic*, as applied to those men who determined to choose Christ as their portion, is first found in the writings of Clement of Alexandria.[2] Like the Virgins, the Ascetis also practiced perfect continence, and voluntary poverty.[3]

Just as the religious life owes its inception to the Virgins and Ascetics of the early years of the Church, so also must one go back to the same Apostolic ages for the first indications of religious profession. It is true that in those early centuries it will be impossible to discover profession so well defined, and so minutely regulated, as it exists in the religious institutes of the present day. It required many centuries of development; in fact, it was not until the present Code of Canon Law was promulgated in 1917 that certain points of profession legislation were finally settled. Cardinal Gasquet has said that "hitherto legislation in regard to religious has been in what may be called a 'fluid state'. It was mostly based upon special Pontifical Constitutions and deductions from the same, and had not hitherto been gathered together and coordinated officially."[4] However, foreshadowings of profession appear already in the early centuries. The Virgins and Ascetics, having once entered upon a life of perfection, felt a determination to persevere. This determination, as time went on, resolved itself into the form of a promise, forming in this manner the background for religious profession. In its broadest sense, therefore, profession may be said to have had its origin in the earliest ages of the Church. No historical documentary evidence, however, can be advanced to show with any degree of certainty whether or not the Virgins and Ascetics

communautés chrétiennes et se retirer dans la solitude. C'est une première étape dans l'évolution de l'ascêtisme vers la form sociale du monachisme..." —Berliere, *L'Ordre Monastique*, p. 23; cf. also Murphy, *St. Basil and Monasticism*, p. 8.

[1] Vermeersch, "Religious Life," *Cath. Encycl.*, XII, 750.

[2] *Paedagog.* I, 7;—*MPL*, VIII, 320.

[3] Besse, *Moines d'Orient*, pp. 21–22; Schiwietz, "Das Mönchtum der ersten drei Christl. Jahrh.", *AkKR*, 78 (1898), 17.

[4] Augustine, *Commentary*, III, iii.

bound themselves by formal, express vow to persevere in the life which they had chosen.[1] It seems rather that during the first, and a great part of the second centuries there existed more of a *propositum* than a formal vow. But already in the latter half of the second century evidence, pointing to a vow, is found in the writings of the Fathers.[2] The first of the Fathers to give such evidence is Clement of Alexandria (150–215). In his *Stromata*[3] he calls virginity a despising of the body in consequence of a promise made to God. In this same work[4] he says that he, who with a determination not to marry has vowed virginity, should remain unmarried.

Origen (185–254) also speaks of a vow or oath to persevere in chastity. In his homily on *Leviticus*, he says: "When we come to God and vow (*vovemus*) to serve Him in chastity...we swear (*juramus*) to chastise our flesh." He adds: "Therefore, any one, if he has sworn (*juravit*) this, and has not kept his vow, becomes guilty of sin."[5] From this it may be seen that already toward the end of the second century the determination, or intention whereby the Virgins and Ascetics proposed to persevere in their chosen life of perfection, was considered to have the same obligatory force, and to cause the same effects as an oath;—the one violating his promise of virginity was deemed guilty of sin.

Tertullian (230), and St. Cyprian (258), in their writings make use of expressions which seem to point to the existence of a vow.[6] Tertullian makes use of the expression *spondere maturitatem*[7], while St. Cyprian employes such phrases as *Christo se dedicare, carne et mente se Deo vovere.*[8]

[1] Schaefer, *Das Ordensrecht*, p. 6; Heimbucher, *Die Orden und Kongregationen*, I, 58–59.

[2] Steiger, "De Propagatione et Diffusione vitae religiosae," *Periodica*, XIII (1924), 40, 41; Schiwietz, "Das Mönchtum der ersten drei Christl. Jahrh.", *AkKR*, 78 (1898), 20.

[3] III, 1—*MPG*, VIII, 1103.

[4] III, 15—*MPG*, VIII, 1197.

[5] "...nos ergo cum venimus ad Deum, et vovemus ei nos in castitate servire, pronuntiamus labiis nostris et juramus nos castigare carnem nostram... Si quis, ergo, hoc juravit et non fecerit peccati efficitur reus."—*Homil. in Levit.* n. 196,—*MPG*, XII, 428.

[6] Schiwietz, "Das Mönchtum der ersten drei Christl. Jahrh.", *AkKR*, 78 (1897), 20.

[7] *De Velandis Virginibus*, c. 6—*MPL*, II 911.

[8] *De Habit. Virg.*, cap. 4—*MPL*, IV, 443–444.

Although from the information gleaned from the writings of these early Fathers of the Church, it can be seen that a vow was in existence among the Virgins and Ascetics as early as the latter half of the second century, it was not until the fourth century that any external ceremony took place in the making of these vows.[1] But toward the middle of this century the taking of vows on the part of the Virgins began to be enhanced with pomp and external solemnity. It was about this time that a change of garb and the investiture with the veil became recognized as specific signs of this act of profession. St. Ambrose (340–397) is the first of the patristic writers to give testimony to this fact. In his *De Virginibus* he refers to this profession as designated by a change of garment.[2] He indicates also that this ceremony was a public one. The profession generally took place on the more solemn feasts of the Church, such as the feast of Easter,[3] Epiphany, and on the feasts of the Apostles.[4] This ceremony was performed before the altar during the Divine Services.[5] The celebrant placed his right hand upon the head of the candidate, and after having recited an appropriate oration, he presented the Virgin with the blessed veil.[6]

What has been said of the vows of the Virgins cannot be applied to those of the Ascetics. Not only are there no indications in the writings of the Fathers pointing to a public ceremony in connection with the profession made by them, but on the contrary, public profession among the Ascetics was denied by these early writers. In the third century they had, as yet, no distinctive garb, on account of which they were severely criticized

---

[1] Koch, *Virgines Christi*, p. 75; Schaefer, *Die Kanonissenstifter*, pp. 38–39.

[2] "...virginitatis professionem vestis quoque mutatione signaris...", Lib. III, cap. 1.—*MPL*, XVI, 219.

[3] "Venit paschae dies, in toto orbe...velantur virgines..."—St. Ambrose, *Exhortatio Virginum*, Cap. 7, n. 42—*MPL*, XVII, 348.

[4] Gelasius I, Const. "*Necessaria rerum*"—*Bull. Rom.*, I, 104.

[5] Heimbucher, *Die Orden und Kongregationen*, I, 58.

[6] "...stabant ad aram Dei pudoris hostia, victima castitatis; nunc capite dextram sacerdotis imponens, precem poscens..."—St. Ambrose, *De Virginibus*, lib. I, cap. 9—*MPL*, XVI, 206; *Canones Synodi Romani*, c. I.—*Mansi*, III, 1134.

by Tertullian.[1] In the earliest monastic communities there is likewise no indication of public profession to be found.[2]

Article 2

PROFESSION IN THE EARLY MONASTIC COMMUNITIES

§1 St. Anthony

St. Anthony was born in Comon, in the northern part of Egypt, about the year 251. His parents died when he was about eighteen or twenty years of age, whereupon Anthony began to lead the life of a hermit. At the age of thirty-five he repaired to the desert. He died on January 17, 356, at the advanced age of 105 years.[3]

St. Anthony was, to a great extent, instrumental in the early development of religious life. The renown of his virtues caused many to seek his companionship in order to become his disciples. These, urged on by a like desire for perfection, settled near the Saint, some living in nearby caves, others in huts in the immediate vicinity. From these disciples, St. Anthony formed his first community about the year 305.[4] Under the guidance of St. Anthony, these disciples faithfully observed the Evangelical Counsels; but one cannot speak of any religious profession made by any of them upon entering the community.[5] It was their own desire and love of chastity, poverty, and obedience that led them to the desert; and it was their determination to persevere, that bound them to practice these virtues.

§2 In the Rule of St. Pachomius

St. Pachomius (292–346) may be called the founder of the coenobitical form of monasticism,[6] and the father of monastic

[1] Cf. Schiwietz, "Das Mönchtum der ersten drei Christl. Jahrh.",—*AkKR*, 78 (1898), 308.

[2] Thomassinus, *Vetus et Nova Eccl. Discip.*, pars I, lib. III, cap. 48, n. 3.

[3] Heimbucher, *Die Orden und Kongregationen*, I, 32–34; Allies, *The Monastic Life*, p. 54.

[4] Heimbucher, *loc. cit.;* Murphy, *St. Basil and Monasticism*, p. 9.

[5] Thomassinus, *Vetus et Nova Eccl. Discipl.*, pars I, lib. III, cap. 48, n. 3.

[6] Smith, *Christian Monasticism*, p.24; Berliere, *L'Ordre Monastique*, p. 25.

rules. He established his community at Tabennisi, on the banks of the Nile. His mode of life differed from that of the anchorites in this, that he arranged his disciples into groups or "folds." They lived under one roof, with strict subjection to a leader. His rule, which was the first written guide for a monastic community, accurately determined the manner of living which was to be followed by those who had placed themselves under his direction. It prescribed community life within the monastic limits, under obedience, and poverty.[1]

In the fourteenth chapter of this rule, St. Pachomius treats of the admission of candidates into his community.[2] In this chapter he gives the necessary directions in reference to the reception, probation, and final admission of candidates into the community. Not all who applied were granted admission.[3] Only those who were considered fit for monastic life who were free from all obligations and worldly ties. Those who had committed crimes, and desired to enter the monastery as refugees from prosecution were likewise denied admittance. But not only negative qualifications were demanded of the candidates. Applicants who were found to possess the required qualifications were first instructed in the monastic discipline; they were taught the things they would be obliged to do; whom they would have to obey. After the time of probation was completed, and the

[1] Cf. *Regula S. Pachomii—MPL*, XXIII, 61 sq.; Piontek, *De Indulto Exclaustrationis necnon Saecularizationis*, p. 16; Schaaf, *The Cloister*, pp. 11–12; Bakalaraczyk, *De Noviatu*, p. 12; Fortescue, "Monasticism," *Cath. Encycl.*, XII, 468; Vermeersch, "Religious Life," *Cath. Encycl.*, XII, 750.

[2] "Si quis accesserit ad ostium monasterii volens sæculo renuntiare, et fratrum aggregare numero non habebit intrandi libertatem, sed prius nuntiabitur Patri monasterii, et manebit paucis diebus foris ante januam, et docebitur orationem dominicam ac psalmos, quantos poterit ediscere; et diligenter sui experimentum dabit, ne forte mali quidpiam fecerit et turbatus ad horam timore discesserit, aut sub aliqua potestate sit; et utrum possit renuntiare parentibus et propriam contemnere facultatem. Si eum viderint aptum ad orationem et ad omnia tunc docebitur et reliquas monasterii disciplinas quas servare debeat et facere, quibus servire, sive in collecta omnium fratrum, sive in domo cui tradendus est, sive in vescendi ordine; ut instructus atque perfectus in omni opere bono, fratribus copuletur. Tunc nudabunt eum vestimentis sæcularibus et induent habitu monachorum, tradentque ostiario, ut orationis tempore adducat eum in conspectum omnium fratrum; sedebitque in loco in quo ei præceptum fuerit."—*Loc. cit.*

[3] Allies, *The Monastic Life*, p. 3.

aspirant was well instructed in the monastic duties; after he had become perfect in good works, he was joined to the monastic community. St. Pachomius then describes how this final adnittance into the ranks of the monks was to take place; the candidate was to change his secular garments for the monastic habit; and at the time of prayer he was to be brought to the assembled community.[1]

The rule makes no reference whatsoever to an explicit vow or profession. The change of garments is the only external formality connected with admission.[2] Although no formal profession was prescribed, there are, however, definite indications of tacit profession, signified by this investiture with the monastic habit. By their entering the community, and by their accepting the monastic habit, they tacitly bound themselves to live the life of chastity, poverty and obedience as demanded by the rule.

§3 Schenute

Schenute was born at Schenalolet, in the district of Akhim.[3] The exact year of his birth is unknown, but it took place somewhere between the years 332 and 350. In the year 371 he became a monk in a monastery called DEIR-EL-ABIAD (White Monastery), near the village of Atripe. His uncle, Bgol, was the abbot of this monastery. After the death of his uncle, Schenute became the community's superior, a position which he held until the time of his death, which occurred about the year 451 or 452.

The rule of St. Pachomius formed the basis of government for the monks under Schenute[4], but he introduced various changes into this rule. A very important change, having bearing on the

[1] "Upon his entrance into the cenobium, each monk voluntarily assumes the obligations of the rule established by St. Pachomius, which specifically required the three great external renunciations of Poverty, Chastity, and Obedience. He receives in return the monastic habit, and enrollment in the order of monks."—Murphy, *St. Basil and Monasticism*, p. 10.

[2] Schiwietz, "Geschichte und Organisation der Pachomianischen Klöster im 4ten Jahrh."—*AkKR*, 82 (1902), 454; Bakalarczyk, *De Noviatu*, p. 13; Steiger, "De Propagatione et Diffusione Vitae Religiosae,"—*Periodica*, XIII (1924), 48; Piontek, *De Indulto Exclaustrationis necnon Sæcularizationis*, p. 17.

[3] Ott, "Schenute," *Cath. Encycl.*, XIII, 527.

[4] Piontek, *De Indulto Exclaustrationis necnon Sæcularizationis*, p. 19.

present subject, was made in the requirements for the admission of candidates. They were first demanded to renounce claim to all property and other possessions, and in the second place, upon joining the community, were obliged to make a verbal promise to strive after perfection. "At no time," Schenute declared, "may any one enter this community to become a monk, without renouncing his possessions, and making his promise before the altar."[1]

The renunciation of property demanded by Schenute had to be drawn up in writing so that a written evidence to the fact would be at hand should any trouble later on arise in questions of inheritance. The promise or oath, which the candidate was obliged to make upon entrance declaring his earnest determination to strive after perfection, had to be made according to a prescribed formula.[2] It must be noted that this formula made no mention of the Evangelical Counsels; it enjoined only the ordinary duties which are demanded of every Christian. As to its effects, it does not expressly bind for life, but Schenute, in his writings, was very much averse to monks leaving the monastic life once they had made the promise. This promise is the first indication to be found of any prescribed formula having been used for admission of candidates into a religious community. The formula, however, was not drawn up in writing; the promise was made orally.[3]

§4 In the Rule of St. Basil

St. Basil the Great was born in Caesaria, in Cappadocia, about the year 329 or 330.[4] After spending the early years of his

---

[1] Cf. Leipoldt, *Schenute von Atripe*, p. 106.

[2] Leipoldt, *loc. cit.*, Ott; (*Cath. Encycl.*, XIII, 527) gives this translation of the oath:

"I vow before God in His holy place, as the word of my mouth is witness: I shall not sully my body in any way: I shall not steal; I shall not take false oaths; I shall not lie; I shall not do evil secretly. If I transgress what I have sworn, I shall not enter the kingdom of heaven, for I know that God, before Whom I pronounce the formula of this pledge will thrust me, body and soul, into hell fire, for I shall have transgressed the formula of the pledge which I have pronounced."

[3] Leipoldt, *Schenute von Atripe*, p. 110–111; Piontek, *De Indulto Exclaustrationis necnon Sæcularizationis*, p. 19.

[4] "Basilius," *Kirchenlexicon*, II,24; "Basil the Great." *Cath. Encycl.*, II,331.

life in the pursuit of knowledge, he determined to enter upon monastic life. With this end in view, he traveled through Syria, Mesopotamia, and Egypt, in order to acquaint himself with the customs of the various monasteries. He returned to his native country, and founded his own community at Pontus, on the banks of the Iris. In the year 370 he was appointed bishop of Caesarea. After laboring faithfully for the flock entrusted to his are, he was called to his reward January 1, 379.

St. Basil left two monastic rules to direct his disciples along the paths of virtue. These are known as the *Regulæ Fusius Tractatæ* and the *Regulæ Brevius Tractatæ*.[1] They were written in a catechetical form; the disciple places the question to which the master gives the answer. Neither of these rules embodies a systematic plan for a monastic community; they contain rather ethical principles and rules of life.[2]

In the fifteenth chapter of the *Regulæ Fusius Tractatæ* St. Basil treats of the reception of candidates. After giving directions for their admission and probation, he regulates the final admittance of these novices into the monastic family.[3] Profession, St. Basil here decrees, is to be preceded by a time of probation, during which the candidate is to be tried in order to ascertain if he is prepared to practice the virtues necessary for monastic life. Only after having given ample proof of his fitness for the life of a monk, is the candidate admitted to profession. (*tunc admittenda est virginitatis professio*). St. Basil speaks here only of chastity, but in various places throughout the two rules he enjoins also obedience[4] and poverty.[5] Profession has to be

---

[1] *MPG*, XXXI, 890–1051.

[2] Zoeckler, *Askese und Mönchtum*, p. 287.

[3] "...Tunc...admittenda est virginitatis professio, tamquam quæ jam sit firma, et quæ ab ipsorum sententia ac judicio proficiscatur jam perfecta et absoluta ratione...Testes autem hujus propositi adhibendi sunt ecclesiarum præfecti...et firma sit hæc actio post multam indigationem ac deliberationem, quam ei licere debet privatim facere dierum plurimum spatio, ne quid per raptum a nobis fieri videatur, ita demum suscipiendus, et inter fratres annumerandus, eandem deinceps et domum et diaetam habiturus cum majoribus..." —*Regul. Fus. Tract.* cap. 15.

[4] *Reg. fus. tract:* cc. 31, 41; *reg. brev. tract;* cc. 9, 115, 117, 118, 119. Cf. Murphy, *St. Basil and Monasticism*, pp. 35–51.

[5] *Reg. brev. tract;* cc. 85, 87, 89, 90, 91, 93, 205. Cf. Murphy, *St. Basil and Monasticism*, pp. 52–61.

made in public, before witnesses; these witnesses were to be the superiors. In order to guard against hasty profession, St. Basil directs that it be made only after due reflection and deliberation. This profession, moreover, marks the entrance of the candidate into the community; before the profession—during the time of probation—he was not yet considered to be a member of the monastic society (*ita demum suscipiendus et inter fratres annumerandus*). The profession likewise placed the candidate on an equal basis with the other members of the community.

No definite age was required for admission into the community. When speaking of this point, St. Basil said that even a very early age was suitable for receiving those who applied for admission; but he also stated that profession can be safely made at that age which is considered suitable for contracting marriage.[1]

The directions for admission to profession, found in the fifteenth chapter of St. Basil's rule, show a marked development in the important act of religious life when compared with the prescriptions laid down in the rule of St. Pachomius. The latter required only tacit profession. St. Basil, on the other hand, prescribed that profession be express;[2] it took place during a public ceremony in the presence of the entire community.

§5 In the Rule of St. Benedict

St. Benedict was born at Nursia in Umbria in the year 480.[3] At an early age he betook himself to Subiaco, where for three years he lived the life of a hermit, secluded in a cave in the mountain. When the fame of his virtues became known, many came desiring to become his disciples. Later on he established twelve monastic communities at Subiaco, but later, about the year 520, he transferred these communities to Monte Cassino. It was here that he later wrote his rule.

St. Benedict divided his rule into seventy-three chapters. In the fifty-eighth he gives instructions for the reception and

---

[1] *Reg. fus. tract.*, cap. 15.

[2] Bakalarczyk, *De Novitiatu*, p. 19; Piontek, *De Indulto Ecxlaustrationis necnon Sæcularizationis*, p. 23.

[3] For a lengthly discussion on the probable dates in the life of St. Benedict, confer Chapman, *St. Benedict and the Sixth Century*, pp. 125–146.

profession of novices. An entire year of probation is prescribed before the novice may be admitted to make his profession. During this year he is to be taught all that is hard and rugged on the way to perfection (*dura et aspera per quæ itur ad Deum*). At stated intervals the rule must be read so that the novice may become fully acquainted with the requirements and duties of a religious. If after this year of trial and preparation the novice feels himself able to observe the precepts of the rule, he may be admitted into the community by profession.

In this same chapter he describes also very minutely the manner of making profession.[1] It is to take place in the oratory as a public act, witnessed by the entire community. The novice must draw up this profession in writing, in the form of a petition. If, however, the novice be unable to write, he must request another to write this petition for him; to this then the novice must affix his mark, generally the sign of the cross. Finally the novice is directed to place the written document upon the altar, thereby signifying his complete renunciation of self, and his perfect union with God.

St. Benedict, in this chapter on profession, lays down a twofold requirement; the verbal promise or vow, and a written document bearing witness that the novice has made the required vows. This written document as required by St. Benedict, is an entirely new feature in the history of religious profession. It is quite certain that St. Benedict was the first to make such a requirement.[2] The document was preserved in the archives of the monastery, to be used against the novice should he afterwards forsake the life he had vowed to lead.

---

[1] "Suscipiendus autem in oratorio coram omnibus promittat de stabilitate sua, et conversione morum suorum, et obedientia, coram Deo et Sanctis ejus, ut si aliquando aliter fecerit, ab Eo se damnandum sciat, quem irridet...De qua promissione sua faciat petitionem ad nomen sanctorum quorum reliquiæ ibi sunt, et Abbatis præsentis. Quem petitionem manu sua scribat, aut si non scit litteras, alter ab eo rogatus scribat, et ille novitius signum faciat, et manu sua eam super altare ponat...Illam...petitionem ejus quam de super altare Abbas tulit, non recipiat, sed in monasterio reservetur."—*Reg. S. Benedicti*, cap. 58.

[2] "Der Organisator des abendländischen Mönchtums ist, so weit wir wissen, der erste, der von dem Novizen eine in aller Form Rechtens ausgestellte Urkunde über die Ablegung seiner Klostergelübde fordert."—Herwegen, *Geschichte der Benediktinischen Professformel*, p. 7.

a) *The Promissio*

It is uncertain whether this promise was made as a simple declaration, or if it was made in the form of questions and answers,[1] as was at one time the prevalent custom of the civil court procedure of Rome. Neither method is excluded from the wording of the rule. The rule prescribes that the novice promise stability, conversion of morals, and obedience. It is again uncertain whether St. Benedict here set down the exact verbal formula according to which the novice was to make his profession, or whether he inserted the words *promittat de stabilitate sua et conversione morum suorum, et obedientia,* merely as a rubric.[2]

Explicitly, the Benedictine novice vows stability, conversion of morals and obedience. St. Benedict distinguished four kinds of monks.[3] The Cenobites, who live in community life, under the direction of an abbot; the Anchorites or Hermits, who single-handed, fight the spiritual battles of life; the Sarabites, who live together in small groups of three or four, without a leader, calling that good and holy which pleases their fancy, while that which is difficult and displeasing, they reject as evil; a final class he calls Gyrovagi, or Wanderers, because they travel from one community to another; they are always wandering, never settled, never satisfied. To guard his disciples against following the evil examples of the Sarabites and Gyrovagi, and to dissuade weaker souls from entering upon the difficult life of the Anchorites, St. Benedict decreed that his monks should make the vow of stability, binding themselves to remain in the community of which they became members by profession.

By the vow of conversion of morals, the Benedictine obliges himself to strive constantly after a higher degree of perfection. Religious life is a state of perfection to be acquired. St. Benedict makes the striving after perfection a matter of vow, thus emphasizing the importance of this phase of religious life.

In this chapter of the rule, St. Benedict makes no illusion to either chastity or poverty. The novice, however, promises obedience according to the rule. In this rule, St. Benedict pre-

---

[1] Rothenhaeusler, *Zur Aufnahmeordnung der Regula S. Benedicti,* p. 3.
[2] *Ibid.* p. 4.
[3] *Regula S. P. Benedicti,* cap. 1.

scribes both chastity and poverty, so that by vowing obedience according to the rule, the Novice implicitly makes also these two essential vows.

To poverty, St. Benedict devoted the entire thirty-third chapter, which bears the heading: "Whether the brethren should have anything of their own." In the very first sentence of this chapter he says that "this vice of ownership must be cut off by the very root." No one, without the command of the Abbot, may presume to receive or to possess anything. Chastity is mentioned in several places in the rule. In the fourth chapter, which contains the "instruments of good works," St. Benedict directs that the monk should "not commit adultery;" that he should "dash against Christ the evil thoughts which may arise in the heart;" that he should "love chastity." The virtue of chastity is again mentioned in the seventh chapter, on humility.

The promise or vow which the novice makes at the end of the time of probation is final and perpetual: "*Suscipiatur in con gregatione sciens...quod ei ex illa die non liceat egredi de monasterio, nec collum excutere de sub jugo Regulæ...*"[1]

b) *The Petitio*

The second requirement established by St. Benedict for the profession is the written document which he called a *petitio*. This document had to be written by the novice, or if he was unable to write, he was obliged to have another write it for him; in this case, the novice had to affix his mark.

The written document, as required by St. Benedict, was more than a mere written formula of the profession; it was what he had called it—a petition or request.[2] Such a form of petition was commonly used in the time of St. Benedict in both the ecclesiastical and civil legal proceedings. Thus, for instance, requests submitted to the Holy See were called *petitiones*,[3] and similarly, a request sent to the emperor had to be in the legal form of a *petitio*.[4] So also the *petitio* prescribed by St. Benedict was a request for admission into the monastic community. It

[1] *Regula S. Benedicti*, cap. 58.
[2] Rothenhaeusler, *Zur Aufnahmeordnung der Regula S. Benedicti*, p. 9, sqq.
[3] Rothenhaeusler, *op. cit.*, p. 10.
[4] Cf. *Cod. Theodosianus*, X, 10, 21.

was at the same time the authentic record of the profession made by the novice.[1] Just what particular formula was used for this *petitio* at the time of St. Benedict can no longer be ascertained. The fundamental elements of the formula, however, are expressed by the words: *promittat de stabilitate, et conversione morum suorum, et obedientia,* of the fifty-eighth chapter of the rule. In his instructions concerning this *petitio,* St. Benedict adheres to the prescriptions of the civil legislation of his time. Thus if the novice himself writes the petition, no subscription is required; but in case another, at the request of the novice, writes it out, the novice must affix his mark. These details are all in accordance with the legal prescriptions of the period.[2]

Article 3

RECAPITULATION

Religious life had its origin in the earliest ages of the Christian era. In the beginning, however, there was no community life; the Virgins and Ascetics strove to practise the Evangelical Counsels without banding themselves into communities. Gradually, community life began to spring up and to flourish. Profession in these early ages of religious life was still undefined. It was, however, foreshadowed in the determination whereby the early Virgins and Ascetics undertook to persevere in the life they had chosen. In the course of time this determination or propositum resolved itself into a private vow. About the middle of the fourth century the act, whereby the Virgins bound themselves to follow Christ in perfect chastity, began to be enhanced with public solemnities. A change of garb and the taking of the veil became distinctive signs of this act of profession.

When, later on, religious life grew into an organization under the leadership of St. Pachomius, profession began to be more defined and determined. Certain qualifications were required of the prospective religious. A term of probation, indefinite though it was, was likewise prescribed before final admission into the

[1] Rothenhaeusler, *op. cit.,* p. 11.

[2] Cf. Cod. VIII, 17, 11; Cod. VIII, 53, 31.

monastic family was granted. The profession act in the rule of St. Pachomius was a more or less private act. A change of secular garment for the monastic habit was the only external sign showing that the novice had taken upon himself the obligations of the religious state.

A step forward was made by St. Basil. By the rule of St. Basil, a term of probation, still indefinite, was prescribed. The candidate was tried and instructed until he was found well fitted to enter upon monastic life. Profession in the rule of St. Basil was more determined that it was in the rule of St. Pachomius. The act of profession was an explicit, public one, it took place before the superiors as witnesses of the profession. Like profession in the rule of St. Pachomius, so also in the rule of St. Basil, it was perpetual.

The rule of St. Benedict goes still farther in determining and regulating this important act of every religious. The time of probation was to extend over a period of one year. In the rule of St. Benedict, profession was a public act. It took place in the oratory, before the entire assembled community. A new feature which was introduced by St. Benedict was the written formula or *petitio*, which he required of every one who made profession. As understood by St. Benedict, profession was perpetual.

CHAPTER III

DEVELOPMENT OF PROFESSION THROUGH ECCLESIASTICAL LEGISLATION

The development of Religious Profession thus far described was brought about by the customs and private regulations of the various religious communities. As time went on, ecclesiastical legislation concerning points of religious profession became necessary in order to bring uniformity into this important phase of religious life, as well as to correct abuses and to effect the stability which is so essential to monastic life. In consequence, the history of profession now becomes the history of positive legislation on this subject. The legislation centers about the main phases of profession, namely, the mode of making profession, its nature and its duration.

Article 1

EXPRESS AND TACIT PROFESSION

Until a comparatively recent date, two valid modes or methods of making profession were acknowledged by the Church. These were express and tacit profession.[1]

Profession is express when the consent of the person making it is manifested by means of word of mouth, or by a written document, or by some similar external sign, explicitly significant of this manifestation of consent.[2] Benedict XIV stated that profession is express when the three vows of religion: chastity, poverty, and obedience are made with the proper prescribed

[1] Suarez, *De Statu Perfectionis et Religionis*, lib. VI, cap. L, n. 7; Reiffenstuel, *Jus Canonicum Universum*, lib. III, tit. XXXI, n. 158; Vecchiotti, *Institutiones*, lib. II, cap. 9; Grandclaude, *Jus Canonicum*, lib. III, pars IV, tit. XXXI, n. 1.

[2] Schmalzgrueber, *Jus Ecclesiasticum Universum*, pars IV, tit. XXXI, n. 155; Reiffenstuel, *op. cit.* lib. III, tit. XXXI, n. 158; Molitor, *Religiosi Juris Capita Selecta*, p. 147.

solemnities, as required by the constitutions of the order or congregation for which the novice makes his profession.[1]

Besides this formal, explicit mode of making profession, there was another way of binding oneself by the vows of religion, and of attaching oneself to a religious community. This mode was the so-called tacit or presumed profession. In this form of profession no formal words were spoken, no explicit solemnities, or acts intrinsically significant of profession took place.[2] Certain acts, however, when performed under certain circumstances were considered as a sufficient manifestation of a novice's intention of living the life of a religious and of binding himself by the religious vows. If, therefore, the novice so acted as to manifest his intention of binding himself to the observance of the vows, without, however, making express, formal profession, such a novice was said to have made tacit profession,[3] since by his external behavior he tacitly manifested his internal intent.[4]

Authorities on Canon Law before the Code, generally admitted three ways in which tacit or presumed profession could take place:[5] 1. By wearing the religious habit for an entire year, provided that there existed in the monastery no distinction between the habit of the novices, and that of the professed religious. 2. If there existed such a distinction of habit, it was required—in the supposition of a tacit profession—that the novice wore the habit proper to the professed religious for a period of three years. In this latter case it was not, however, necessary that the time of probation be already completed before the novice donned the habit of the professed. 3. Another instance in which tacit pro-

---

[1] Const. "*Anno Vertente*," 19 June 1750—*Bull. de Prop. Fide*, III, 270.

[2] Schmalzgrueber, *op. cit.* pars IV, tit. XXXI, n. 155; Reiffenstuel, *op. cit.* lib. III, tit. XXXI, n. 177; Rodericus, *Quæstiones Regulares*, CI, n. 53; Molitor, *Religiosi Juris Cap. Selecta* p. 147.

[3] Benedict XIV, const. "*Anno Vertente*," June 19, 1750—*Bull. de Prop. Fide*, III, 270.

[4] "Professio tacita non dicitur ob solum taciturnitatem, quasi ex sola consensus præsumi possit, id enim verum non est, quia in præjudicialibus sola taciturnitas, etiam scientis et præsentis, non habetur pro consensu...sed præterea requiritur actus positivus, qui vel ex rei natura, vel ex juris dispositione significet consensum..."—Pirhing, *Jus Canonicum*, lib. iii, tit. XXXI, n. 113.

[5] Reiffenstuel, *Jus Canonicum Universum*, lib. III, tit. XXXI, n. 177; Schmalzgrueber, *Jus. Eccl. Universum*, pars IV, tit. XXXI, n. 156; Suarez, *De Statu Perfectionis et Religionis*, lib. IV, cap. 19, n. 3.

fession could become effective, arose when the novice performed some act which was reserved to one already professed. Such acts were, for example, to take part in chapter proceedings, to cast a vote in chapter. To assume the office of abbot was also equivalent to making tacit profession. In order that tacit profession could take place by the performance of such acts, it was not necessary that the habit of the professed (where such a distinction existed) be worn for a period of three years before the tacit profession could become effective; on the contrary, by the very fact that a novice performed such an act reserved to professed religious, tacit profession became effective. But in order that one make tacit profession by the performance of any of these reserved acts, it was necessary that the individual had been validly received into the novitiate by investiture with the religious habit.[1]

In order that tacit profession could be considered valid and binding, several conditions had to be complied with. It was first required that the consent of the superior be had, who was empowered to receive the profession of a novice.[2] Since, as was shown above, profession is a contract, it is necessary that the consent of both parties to the contract be given; on the part of the superior, the consent is manifested by accepting the profession of a candidate for the order. Therefore, unless a profession be accepted by the legitimately constituted superior, such a profession is non-existing. This was shown by the fact that Alexander II declared a profession null because it had not been accepted by a compentent superior.[3] The same was declared to be the case by Alexander III (1159–1181) in a letter to the Bishop of Lugo.[4]

A second condition required for the validity of tacit profession was, that the novice be aware of the fact that by wearing the monastic habit for the required period of time, or that by performing an act proper only to a professed religious, tacit pro-

---

[1] Schmalzgrueber, *Jus. Eccl. Univ.* pars IV, tit. XXXI, n. 156; Reiffenstuel, *Jus. Canonicum Univ.*, lib. III, tit. XXXI, n. 177; Suarez, *De Statu Perfectionis et Religionis*, lib. VI, cap. 19, n. 7; Augustine, *Commentary*, III, 256.

[2] Reiffenstuel, *Jus Canonicum Universum*, lib. III, tit. XXXI, n. 180; Schmalzgrueber, *Jus Ecclesiasticum Universum*, pars IV, tit. XXXI, n. 157; Gonzalez, *Commentarium*, lib. III, tit. XXXI, cap. XIII, n. 5.; Rodericus, *Quæstiones Regulares*, CI, n. 53.

[3] C. 1, C. XXVII, q. 2.

[4] C. 4, X, *Qui clerici vel voventes, etc.*, IV, 6.

fession would result.[1] The voluntary consent of the parties of any contract is necessary for its validity; so likewise for religious profession. But the novice could not have given his free consent if he had been ignorant of the fact that an act he performed under certain circumstances was tantamount to tacit profession. It was, however, presumed that the novice possessed this required knowledge, unless the contrary could be proved.

A further requirement for the validity of tacit profession was that the novice perform the act from which the tacit profession could result, with the intention of binding himself, which intention was presumed to be present unless circumstances proved otherwise. It was finally required that the novice act freely, without coercion, without unjustly inflicted fear.[2]

Tacit profession had the very same binding force, it entailed the same obligations, as resulted from express profession.[3] The reason for this was that the novice who, with full knowledge of the circumstances, nevertheless wore the habit for the required period of time, or performed an act proper only to a professed member, was presumed to have acted in this manner with the intention of binding himself forever to the obligations of religious life. This presumption was *juris et de jure*, so that, unless the novice had expressly stated that he had no intention of binding himself, contrary proof would not be admitted.[4]

§1. From the Beginning, up to the Council of Trent —A.D. 1545—

As has already been seen from the analysis of the early history of religious profession, tacit profession was, in the beginning, the common form of profession. It was St. Basil who introduced, and St. Benedict who developed, express profession. From the time of St. Benedict, express profession began to take the place of tacit profession, but not to the exclusion of this latter form. Already in the tenth council of Toledo (656) express, written,

---

[1] Reiffenstuel, *Jus Canonicum Universum*, lib. III, tit. XXXI, n. 180; Rodericus, *Quæstiones Regulares*, CI, n. 53.

[2] Reiffenstuel, *loc. cit.*

[3] Schmalzgrueber, *Jus Eccl. Univ.*, pars IV, tit. XXXI, n. 157; Suarez, *De Statu Perfectionis et Religionis*, lib. VI, cap. 21, n. 2.

[4] Schmalzgrueber, *loc. cit.*

profession was prescribed for women who took the veil.[1] Tacit profession, was not, however, excluded, either by the rule of St. Benedict,[2] or by positive ecclesiastical legislation. On the contrary, many papal letters and decrees attest to both the existence and validity of tacit profession. The fifth council of Orleans (549) declared that maidens who had entered a convent and had received the religious habit, could no longer leave the enclosure.[3] This same legislation was later adopted by the second council of Auvergne.[4] The sixth synod of Toledo, held in 638, declared that any one, either male or female, who had put on the religious habit, could not return to secular life.[5] This same idea was expressed by Pope Eugene II (824–827) in the synod of Rome in 826.[6] Nicholas I (858–867) decreed that a widow who had once placed the veil upon her head, or who had, during divine services, taken a place among the other veiled women, was no longer free to abandon the duties of those who had made religious profession.[7]

A certain bishop complained to Pope Honorius III (1216–1227) that there were in his diocese men who, although they had worn the religious habit for many years, did not make express profession, that they retained their possessions, and lived scandalous lives; as an excuse for their conduct they stated that the religious habit does not make one a monk. The Pope in his answer to the bishop decreed that the latter should compel under pain of ecclesiastical censure all such of his subjects who had worn the religious habit for a period of one year, to observe the obligations and duties of monastic discipline,[8] thus affirming that the wearing of the monastic garb for a stated period of time would induce tacit profession. Pope Gregory IX (1227–1241) also indicated the validity of tacit profession when he said that novices

---

[1] C. 4, *Mansi*, XI, 35.

[2] "Die von der Kirche allgemein als gültig anerkannte stillschweigende Profess gelangte...auch im Benediktinerorden zur Geltung."—Scharnagl, *Das Feierliche Gelübde als Ehehinderniss*, p. 21.

[3] Can. 19, *Mansi*, IX, 133.

[4] Can. 19, *Mansi*, IX, 146.

[5] Can. 6, *Hefele*, III, 90.

[6] C. 31, C. XXVII, q. 1.

[7] *Decr. Nicholai I*, tit. XIII, c. 3.—*Mansi*, XV, 443.

[8] C. 22, X, *de Regularibus et transeuntibus ad Religionem*, III, 31.

may leave the monastery before they receive the habit of the professed;[1] in other words, once they had put on the habit of the professed, egress would be denied them. In the synod of Lambeth (1281) it was decreed that one who had remained in the monastery for more than a year could no longer leave the cloister, even though such a person had made no formal profession.[2] Boniface VIII (1294–1303)[3] and Clement V (1305–1314),[4] likewise bear testimony to the existence and validity of tacit profession.

§2 From the Council of Trent to the Code (1545—1917)

The Council of Trent did much to bring unity and uniformity into some phases of religious profession. Among other regulations, the Council ordained that a minimum age of sixteen years, and an entire year of probation were to be required for the validity of profession.[5] No formal declarations, however, were enacted concerning tacit profession. Hence canonists were of the opinion that this mode of making profession was not abolished by the Council. Their reason was as follows: since the Council changed nothing of the common law of profession, with the exception of establishing the minimum age of sixteen years, and deciding upon an entire year of probation, therefore all other points of former legislation on profession remained unchanged and in force even after the Council.[6] Canonists further agreed that after the Council, in order that tacit profession could validly take place, the enactments of the Council in question, with reference to the required age and probation, had to be observed.[7]

[1] C. 23, X, *de Regularibus et transeuntibus ad Religionem*, III, 31.

[2] C. 19.—*Mansi*, XXIV, 416.

[3] C. 3, *de Regularibus et transeuntibus ad Religionem*, III, 14, in VI°; cap. un., *de Statu Regularium*, III, 16, in VI°; c. 21, *de sententia excommunicationis, suspensionis*, et *interdicti*, V, 11, in VI°.

[4] C. 2, *de Regularibus et transeuntibus ad Religionem*, III, 9, in Clem.

[5] Sess. XXV, *de regul. et monial.*, cap. 15.

[6] Reiffenstuel, *Jus Canonicum Universum*, lib. III, tit. XXXI, n. 178; Schmalzgrueber, *Jus Ecclesiasticum Universum*, pars IV, tit. XXXI, n. 159; Rodericus, *Quæstiones Regulares*, CI, n. 53; Grandclaude, *Jus Canonicum*, lib. III, pars IV, tit. XXXI, n. 1.

[7] Benedict XIV, const. "Anno Vertentet" June 19, 1750, par. 10, *Bullarium de prop. Fide*, III, 270; De Angelis, *Prælectiones J. Canonici*, lib. III, tit. XXXI, p. 106.

An objection to the validity of tacit profession after the Council of Trent can be raised because of the declaration of the sixteenth chapter of the twenty-fifth session. In this chapter it was decreed that when the time of probation has been completed and the novice has attained the required age, he must either be admitted to profession immediately, or be requested to leave the monastery. Rodericus[1] offers an answer to this objection when he says that, although the Council decreed that the novice, if not accepted for profession, must leave the monastery after the term of probation has expired, it does not expressly deny that tacit profession will not take place if the novice nevertheless remains. To this same objection, De Angelis[2] answers that the Council, in the chapter in question, stated a general rule which admits of exceptions. He concludes that if the novice, although not admitted to express profession, is not commanded to leave the monastery, tacit profession may validly take place, provided the other conditions required by the decrees of the Council have been fulfilled.

Further proof that tacit profession was not abolished by the Council of Trent is found in the constitution of Sixtus V "*Ad Romanum spectat*" of the 21 of October, 1588.[3] In this constitution he states:

Sed cum eadem vigeat in tacita professione emittenda quæ militat in expressa statuimus...neque etiam tacita quorumcumque Religiosorum induci possit, nec inducta intelligatur, nisi in receptione constitutionis forma servata fuerit. Hence Schmalzgrueber[4] concludes that if the novice was received in accordance with the regulations of the constitutions of the order he intends to enter, tacit profession could, even after the Council of Trent, validly take place.

During this period, legislation bearing on express profession was issued by the Holy See as time and circumstances demanded. Gregory XIII on November 1, 1579, in an instruction "*Benedictus Dominus*,"[5] demanded that all religious of the Order of St.

---

[1] *Quæstiones Regulares*, CI, n. 53.
[2] *Prælectiones J. Canonici*, lib. III, tit. XXXI, pp. 106, 107.
[3] *Fontes*, n. 164.
[4] *Jus Eccl. Universum*, pars. IV, tit. XXXI, n. 159.
[5] *Bullarium Romanum*, VIII, 309 (par. 8).

Basil must make express profession into the hands of the Abbot or Prior of the Monastery. Clement VIII in his decree "*Cum ad Regularem*,"[1] of March 19, 1603, among other matters, prescribed that every monastery keep a book into which the novices inscribe their profession. The keeping of such a record book of profession did not, however, originate with this decree. Such a book was in existence in the Monastery of St. Gall as early as the ninth century.[2] The synod of Mt. Libanon in 1736, declared that express profession must be made by all monks coming under its jurisdiction. This synod further specified that the profession was to take place in the form of question and answer; the abbot placing the question to which the novice was to respond.[3]

None of this legislation demanding express profession had any effect on the validity of tacit profession. This mode of profession continued to be universally recognized as a valid means for making profession until the latter part of the nineteenth century. The encyclical "*Neminem latet*," issued by Pius IX, on March 19, 1857, decreed that solemn profession in orders of men could in future be made only after the novice had spent a period of three years in simple vows. A subsequent decree of the Congregation in charge of the Affairs of Religious issued, June 12, 1858, under the title "*Sanctissimus*,"[4] declared that in order validly to make solemn profession after the period spent in simple vows, express profession was necessary, and declared, moreover, that for orders of men, tacit profession was abolished.[5] Therefore tacit profession could thereafter no longer be recognized in orders of men in which simple vows were made. The prescriptions of the decree "*Sanctissimus*" did not, however, apply to those institutes of men whose members made only simple profession.[6]

---

1 *Bullarium Romanum*, X, 776 (par. 34).

2 Herwegen, *Geschichte der Benediktinischen Professformel*, p. 33 sqq.

3 "Monachus tria vota...explicite emittit...Abbate interrogante; An velit conservare seipsum in castitate et paupertate et observare obedientiam superiori usque ad mortem, cui Monachus respondet; Ita pater, Domino adjuvante, et precum tuarum præsidio." C.5.—*Coll. Lac.*, II, 373.

4 Bizzarri, *Collect.*, p. 855.

5 "...et ideo tacita professio omnio abrogata est"—decr. "*Sanctissimus*" par. XI, Bizzarri, *Collect.* p. 855.

6 Piat, *Prælectiones Juris Regularis*, I, 142.

In orders of men, therefore, tacit profession as a valid mode of profession, ceased with the promulgation of the decree "*Sanctissimus.*"

In religious orders of women, tacit profession continued to be recognized as a valid mode of making profession. The encyclical "*Neminem latet*" had no reference to orders of women, so that the legislation in force before the publication of this encyclical continued to be the guiding principle for their professions. It was not until the beginning of the twentieth century that a change in legislation for orders of women was made. On May 3, 1902, the Sacred Congregation of Bishops and Regulars issued the decree "*Perpensis*",[1] in virtue of which regulations, similar to those contained in the encyclical "*Neminem latet*", were extended to orders of women. Since the simple vows which were required by the decree "*Perpensis*" were of the same nature as those prescribed for orders of men by the encyclical "*Neminem latet*," the prescriptions of the decree "*Sanctissimus*" were likewise extended to orders of women.[2] Consequently, tacit profession in orders of women, ceased to exist with the publication of the decree "*Perpensis*," on May 3, 1902.

Since neither the decree "*Sanctissimus*" nor the decree "*Perpensis*" effected religious congregations in which only simple vows were made, tacit profession in these institutes was not abrogated until, with the promulgation of the Code, express profession became a requirement for the validity of each and every religious profession.[3]

ARTICLE 2

SOLEMN AND SIMPLE PROFESSION

§1 Historical Background for the Distinction

The terms *solemn* and *simple* vows are found for the first time in the *Decretum Gratiani.*[4] In the various canons of the twenty-seventh distinction in the first part of his decree, he cites

---

[1] *ASS*, XXXV (1902–1903), 31 sq.

[2] Bachofen, *Compendium Juris Regularium*, p. 83.

[3] Can. 572 §1, 5°.

[4] Wernz-Vidal, *Jus Matrimoniale*, p. 353; Ballay, *AkKR*, 17 (1867), 3 sqq; Vermeersch, *De Religiosis*, II, (11).

two views held by the Fathers and Councils concerning the marriages of such who had, before marriage, vowed to live in perpetual chastity. Some such marriages had been declared illicit, but nevertheless valid,[1] while others had been held to be not only illicit, but likewise invalid.[2] Considering these two views on this important question, Gratian comes to the conclusion that there must be a distinction in the vows of these two classes of persons.[3] To this distinction he applies the terms *simple* and *solemn*. These terms, as applied to the two classes of vows by Gratian, was taken up by Bernard[4] and taught in the schools of canon law until they were officially adopted by the Supreme Pontiffs.[5]

Although these terms began to be used only during the twelfth and thirteenth centuries, it is the opinion of many authorities on canon law that the distinction between the vows, which causes some to invalidate subsequent marriages and others to render such a proceeding only illicit, existed *de facto* many centuries before the terms *solemn* and *simple* vows were applied to them. But at the same time, authorities admit that it is very difficult, if not impossible, to ascertain just when religious profession began to have the invalidating effects with reference to marriage it now has. There existed no definite, universal legislation in this matter till the middle of the twelfth century; but at the same time it cannot be denied that individual popes and councils issued decrees and regulations which point rather strongly to the existence of such effects as early as the fifth and sixth centuries.

Already in the time of the early Fathers of the Church the marriages of persons who had vowed perpetual chastity were frowned upon, the parties to such marriages were compared to adulterers and bigamists; but the Fathers, in their writings, did not state definitely that these unions were invalid. St. Cyprian seems rather to consider them to be valid, and in certain cases, even licit. In his sixty-second letter to Pomponius, written about the year 249, he compares virgins, who leave the state of virginity to contract marriage, to adulterous persons. Just as

---

1 C. 2, 3, 5, D. XXVII.
2 C. 8, D. XXVII.
3 Ad. c. 8, D. XXVII.
4 Vermeersch, *De Religiosis*, 11, (10).
5 C. 3, 6, 7, X, *qui clerici vel voventes matrimonium contrahere possunt*, IV, 6.

the husbands, he says, are justly angered if they discover the sinful lives of their consorts, so will Christ, the spiritual Spouse of every virgin, be angered at such who are unfaithful to their vows.[1] But in this same letter he says that if a virgin finds it difficult to persevere in her chosen life it will be better for her to marry.[2] Suarez, commenting on this passage, says that some canonists interpret these words of St. Cyprian to mean that he considers all marriages of virgins to be illicit, but that under certain circumstances such marriages could be tolerated as lesser evils than concubinage. Suarez, however, is opposed to this interpretation, and states that St. Cyprian considers marriage under the given circumstances not only valid, but likewise lawful.[3]

St. Basil is more severe in his denouncement of marriage of persons who had embraced the state of perpetual virginity. He states that those who have vowed virginity, but have afterwards yielded to the temptations of the flesh, try to hide their iniquity under the name of marriage. He seems, however, to consider such marriages to be invalid, because he continues to say that a virgin cannot be considered the wife of him to whom she has been joined through sin.[4] In his second canonical letter, he considers such virgins adulteresses, and says that just as he who lives with a woman not his wife is called an adulterer, and is not admitted to the Church until he has given up his sinful life, so also must those be punished who presume to contract marriage with a virgin.[5] He is more lenient with converts to the true faith. He permits those persons to contract marriage after their conversion who, before they became members of the Church, had vowed to live lives of perpetual chastity.[6]

---

[1] *Ep. 62 ad Pomponium*, c. 3—*MPL*, IV, 368–369.

[2] "...si autem perseverare nolunt vel non possunt, melius est ut nubant quam in ignem delictis suis cadant..." C. 2.—*MPL*, IV, 366–367.

[3] "...aperte concedit Cyprianus illas nuptias non solum ut minus malas sed etiam ut non malas, et honestas."—*De Statu Perfectionis et Religionis*, lib. IX, cap. II, n. 9.

[4] "...cum virginitatem Domino voverint, postea carnis voluptatibus victæ, stupri peccatum matrimonii nomine prætexere volunt: non ignorantes...quamvis ignorantiam præ se ferant, eam...neque illius sponsam esse quem illigitime reliquit, neque illius cui se per libidinem junxit secundum leges uxorem videri posse..."—*De Vera Virgin. Integrit.*, n. 37—*MPG*, XXX, 746.

[5] *Epistola Canonica II*, par. XVIII—*MPG*, XXXI, 719.

[6] *Ibid.*, par. XX,—*MPG*, XXXI, 719.

St. Ambrose declared that a person who has vowed to observe perfect chastity has already contracted a spiritual marriage with Jesus Christ. For such a virgin even to wish to enter an earthly marriage would be adultery; instead of being a spouse of Christ, she would become a handmaid of death.[1]

St. Augustine declared that it is wrong for a professed virgin even to desire marriage.[2] He moreover considers a virgin, who would dare abandon her chosen state of virginity for the marriage state, worse than an adulteress.[3] But that he considers such marriages, even though gravely sinful, to be nevertheless valid, appears from the fact that he says that the parties of such marriages may not be separated.[4]

The writings of the Fathers leave the existence of a vow which could invalidate a subsequent marriage, very doubtful. They all consider the marriages of virgins gravely sinful, even adulterous, but they do not expressly state that such marriages were to be considered as null and void on account of the existing vow of virginity. The decrees of the early councils are equally obscure. The various councils take different views in the matter. Some demand that the guilty parties be severely punished, others that they be separated. None of them, however, explicitly declared such marriages to be invalid. It is, however, very noticeable that the tendency of these councils is to grow more severe in each succeeding century towards the parties of such marriages.

The synod of Valence (347) decreed that virgins who had contracted marriage should be subjected to salutary penances until they had made complete satisfaction.[5] The fourth council of Carthage (398) considers such persons to be deserving of con-

---

[1] "Quæ se spopondit Christo, et sanctam velamen accepit, jam nupsit, jam immortali juncta est viro; etiamsi voluerit nubere communi lege conjugii, adulterium perpetrat, ancilla mortis efficitur..."—*De Laps. Virg.*, cap. 5,—*MPL*, XVI, 373.

[2] "...in virginali et viduali continentia...qua expedita et electa, et voti debito oblata, jam non solum capessere nuptias, sed, etiam si non nubant, nubere velle damnabile est."—*De Bon. Viduit.*, cap. 9,—*MPL*, XL, 437.

[3] "...plane non dubitaverim dicere, lapsus et ruinas a castitate sanctiore, quæ vovetur Deo, adulteriis esse pejores..."—*De Bon. Viduit.*, cap. 11—*MPL*, XL, 439.

[4] Cf. *De Bon. Viduit.*, cap 10—*MPL*, XL, 438.

[5] C. 2—*Mansi*, II, 494.

demnation because they have broken the vows made to God.[1] The same thought was later expressed in the synod of Orange in 441.[2]

Innocent I, in a letter to Victricius, written about the year 404, speaks of two classes of virgins; those who had made only the vow; and those who besides taking the vow, had also received the veil, significant of the state of virginity. When treating of the first class, he says that they should do penance for a short time, if they should presume to give up the state of virginity to enter into a matrimonial contract.[3] But the second class, for the same misdeed, he says, incur excommunication and may not be admitted to do penance in expiation for the crime, until after the death of the party with whom they had contracted the sinful marriage.[4] Pope Innocent, in his letter, indicates that already in the fifth century, the marriage of a virgin who had been veiled was considered to be a graver sin than the marriage of an unveiled virgin. He compares the marriages of veiled virgins to the sinful lives of adulterous women, stating in the twelfth chapter of this same letter that just as the wife, who while her husband is still living, attempts marriage with another man, is said to be an adulteress, and is in consequence, not to be admitted to penitential works until one of the two men has been removed by death, so much the more should this law be enforced against her, who has contracted marriage after having become the spouse of Christ.[5]

A synod held in Ireland, by St. Patrick, about the year 450 or 456, decreed that if persons, bound by religious profession, presume to enter the matrimonial state, they are excommunicated until they repent of their crime; if they dismiss the unlawful partner they may be admitted to the ranks of the penitents; the synod

---

[1] C. 28—*Mansi*, VI, 440.

[2] C. 35, C. XXVII, q. 1.

[3] C. 9, C. XXVII, q. 1.

[4] C. 10, C. XXVII, q. 1.

[5] "Si enim de hominibus hæc ratio custoditur, ut quæcunque vivente viro, alteri nupserit adultera habeatur; nec ei agendæ poenitentiæ licentia concedatur, nisi unus de eis fuerit defunctus, quanta magis de illa tenenda est, quæ ante immortali se sponso conjunxerat, et postea ad humanas nuptias transmigravit?"—c. 10, C. XXVII, q. 1.

adds that they may not again afterwards live together under the same roof.[1]

The Council of Chalcedon (451) is equally severe against such marriages, and proceeds against the guilty parties with excommunication. The Council, however, indicates that under certain circumstances, such marriages could be permitted. The sixteenth canon, which declares the sentence of excommunication against offending persons, adds that the bishop could show mercy to such parties.[2] In view of this last clause, Suarez, although he defends the opinion that already in the early centuries, vows had the power of invalidating marriages, admits the probability of the opposite opinion, which holds that the Council of Chalcedon did not consider marriages of virgins invalid, but only sinful. The bishop, Suarez says, could not show mercy unless the marriages were valid. He continues, however, to say that this decree, "*posse fieri humanitatem,*" may also have reference to absolution from the censure incurred, and not to the cohabitation of the parties.[3]

Pope Leo I,[4] in a letter written about 458 or 459, also treats of this subject. It is his opinion that a monk cannot contract marriage without at the same time becoming guilty of grave sin. Monks who offend in this matter must be subjected to public penances. He does not, however, consider such marriages invalid; in referring to them he says that under certain circumstances they could even be considered lawful.[5] He enjoins penances on offenders, not so much because they have contracted marriage, but because in doing so they deserted a higher good to which they had bound themselves by vow.[6] In a subsequent chapter of the same letter, he speaks in like manner of offending virgins. Such, he says, do wrong even though consecration has not accompanied their profession. There can be no doubt, he says, that offending virgins are guilty of serious sin, if they have received consecration

---

[1] Can. 17—*Mansi*, VI, 518.

[2] "Si...virgo se dedicaverit Deo, similiter monachus, non licet eis nuptiis jungi. Si vero inventi fuerint hoc facientes, maneant excommunicati. Statuimus vero eis posse fieri humanitatem."—c. 22, C, XXVII, q. 1.

[3] *De Statu Perfectionis et Religionis*, lib. IX, cap. XXII, n. 23.

[4] C. 1, C. XX, q. 3.

[5] "...honestum potest esse conjugium," *ibid.*

[6] "...electionem...meliorum deseruisse transgressio est"—*loc. cit.*

at the time of their profession.[1] Pope Leo, in this chapter, distinguishes between consecrated and unconsecrated virgins. When speaking of the marriages of the former, he makes use of the expression, *magnum crimen admitti*, but uses the word *prævaricari* in referring to the marriages of the latter, indicating thereby that the marriages of the consecrated virgins were considered a more serious sin than those of the unconsecrated virgins. In neither case, however, does he indicate the invalidity of such marriages.

Towards the end of the fifth and the beginning of the sixth centuries, more severe legislation was enacted against religious, both male and female, who became unfaithful to their vows. Pope Gelasius I (483–493) expressly prohibited marriage to persons bound by religious profession.[2] The first Council of Orleans (509) decreed that monks who gave up the religious state for marriage, could not receive an ecclesiastical office of any kind.[3]

During the sixth century the decrees of the various councils point somewhat vaguely to the possible existence of vows possessing the power of invalidating subsequent marriage contracts. During this and the following centuries, the councils, with ever increasing frequency, declared that the parties of marriages of whom one is bound by religious profession, must be separated. Some decrees demanded not only the separation of the parties, but required also an oath that they would never thereafter dwell together under the same roof.[4] The Council of Tours (567) decreed that when necessary, the authority of the civil tribunal was to be employed in separating such offending parties.[5]

The fact that the separation of the parties was demanded when one of the contracting persons had made religious profession is, in the opinion of Suarez, a very strong, though no absolute, argument that such marriages were not only illicit, but also invalid.

---

[1] "...ambigi non potest crimen magnum admitti ubi et propositum et consecration violatur..."—C. 8, C. XX, q. 1.

[2] "Neque viduas ad nuptias transire patimur, quæ in religioso proposito diuturna observatione permanserunt. Similiter virgines nubere prohibemus, quas annis plurimis in monasteriis ætatem peregisse contigerit."—C. 3, C. XXVII, q. 1.

[3] C. 1—*Mansi*, VIII, 355.

[4] C. 17, C. XXVII, q. 1.

[5] C. 15—*Hefele*, III, 24.

His reason is that such a separation, if the marriage were valid, would place such parties in grave danger of incontinence. Since moreover, he says, it could very easily happen that the innocent party to such a marriage was in good faith, such separations, if the marriage were valid, would in consequence subject the innocent party to involuntary celibacy without any fault on his part. This, Suarez thinks, would be not only dangerous and burdensome, but also an injustice to the innocent party.[1]

St. Gregory the Great indicates a bit more clearly the possibility of vows having the faculty of causing subsequently attempted marriages to be invalid. In a letter written to Anthemius about the year 591, he demanded that religious who had left the monastic enclosure and had contracted marriage be diligently sought after, and be not only separated from their unlawful partners, but be obliged to return to the monasteries they had forsaken.[2] He makes the same demands in another letter which was written to Bishop Marinianus in 597.[3]

The fourth Council of Toledo (633) also decreed that monks, who left their monasteries and contracted marriage, must return and there expiate their crime by performing salutary penances.[4] This same Council, in its eighth canon, declared that widows and virgins who, contrary to the decrees of the Fathers and the canonical precepts, had entered into marriage contracts, must be excommunicated until they amend.[5]

A synod held in Rome in 721 is very forceful in denouncing one who was guilty of seducing a virgin.[6] A subsequent synod of Rome, held in 743, warns virgins against contracting impious marriages (*nefario conjugio copulare*). If they refused to heed this warning, they were to be excommunicated. But they were permitted to perform penances, providing they consented to separate.[7]

---

[1] *De Statu Perfectionis et Religionis*, lib. IX, cap. XXI, n. 11. The same view is taken by Vidal—Wernz-Vidal, *Jus Matrimoniale*, p. 349, fn. 13.

[2] C. 39, C. XXVII, q. 1.

[3] C. 15, C. XXVII, q. 1.

[4] C. 53—*Hefele*, III, 84.

[5] C. 7, C. XXVII, q. 1.

[6] C. 3 "...si quis monacham, quam Dei ancillam appellamus, in conjugium duxerit, anathema sit." C. 3—*Mansi* XII, 263.

[7] C. 5.—*Mansi*, XII, 383.

Pope Nicholas I (858–867) also demanded that those who had made religious profession, but had afterwards contracted marriage, do penance for their sin; they were obliged, also, to return to the religious community they had deserted.[1] A similar decree was later issued by the Council of Tribur in 895.[2]

From these decrees and from the writings of the Popes, one cannot obtain conclusive evidence that during these centuries religious profession was of such a nature that it formed a diriment impediment to marriage. But, on the other hand, it can hardly be denied that these decrees and canons contain rather plain indications that at least in some localities profession had this invalidating effect. And moreover, as is evident from several of the decrees and papal letters cited above, a distinction was made between one profession and another. The marriages of some professed persons were considered to be a more serious violation than were the marriages of others. In consequence there is some ground for asserting that at least in certain regions, the actual distinction between solemn and simple vows existed before the exact terminology began to be applied to the two kinds of vows. Not a few of the canonists defended this opinion; among them are Suarez,[3] Devoti,[4] and Ballay.[5] It is Surez's opinion that because in these early centuries the government of religious communities was entrusted to the local Ordinaries, it was very easily possible that various local customs and legislations in this matter could have arisen, until a general, universal law was enacted. Devoti thinks that already in the fourth century there existed vows which rendered a subsequent marriage contract invalid, and others which only impeded marriage. He concludes that those seriously err who say that during the first five centuries there existed no vow to which the invalidating power was joined. De-Angelis[6] is of the opposite opinion; he holds that the distinction between simple and solemn vows did not come into existence until shortly before the middle of the eleventh century. Authors

---

[1] "...reverti ad id quod spopondit..."—*Mansi*, XV, 433; c. 6, D. XXVII.

[2] C. 12, 13, C. XXVII, q. 1.

[3] *De Statu Perfectionis et Religionis*, lib. IX, cap. XXI, nn. 26, 27.

[4] *Institutiones*, lib. II, tit. II, sec., 9, n. 129.

[5] "Quæstiones quædam de votis simplicibus," *AkKR*, 17 (1867) 3 sq.

[6] *Prælectiones J. Canonici*, lib. III, tit. XXXI, n. 3.

after the Code can also be found who defend the opinion that already in the early centuries this distinction existed. Among these are Vidal,[1] Chelodi,[2] and Petrovits.[3]

§2 From the I Lateran Council to the Encyclical "Neminem Latet" 1123—1857

The first evidence of any universal legislation which at least implicitly declared that profession invalidated marriage contracted after the profession had been made, is to be found in a canon of the first Lateran Council, held in 1123. The twenty-first canon of this Council forbids marriage to professed men, and moreover declares that those who had contracted marriage must be separated.[4]

Any doubt in this matter, which may still have existed after the First Lateran Council, was finally dispelled by the Second Lateran Council, held under Innocent II, in 1139. The words used by this council in declaring marriages, contracted by parties bound by religious profession, to be both illicit and invalid, leave no room for further doubt. It was very explicit in declaring the marriages of both male and female religious null and void.[5]

The legislation of the First and Second Lateran Councils was reaffirmed by several later Pontiffs; by Alexander III (1159–1181),[6] Innocent III (1198–1266),[7] Boniface VIII (1294–1303),[8] and finally by the decrees of the Council of Trent.[9]

After it had been declared in the First and Second Lateran Councils that the marriages of persons bound by religious pro-

---

[1] Wernz–Vidal, *Jus Matrimoniale*, 352 sqq.

[2] *Jus Matrimoniale*, p. 54.

[3] *New Church Law on Matrimony*, p. 195.

[4] "...monachis...matrimonia penitus interdicimus; contracta quoque matrimona ab hujusmodi personis disjungi...judicamus."—*Mansi*, XXI, 286.

[5] "...statuimus quatenus...monachi atque conversi professi, qui sacntum transgredientes propositum uxores sibi copulare præsumpserint, separentur. Hujusmodi namque copulationem, quam contra ecclesiasticam regulam constat esse contractam, matrimonium non esse censemus...Id ipsum quoque de sanctimonialibus feminis si...nubere attentaverint, observari decernimus."—Cc. 17, 18—*Mansi* XXI, 527–528.

[6] C. 3, X, *qui clerici vel voventes matrimonium contrahere possunt*, IV, 6.

[7] C. 7, X, *qui clerici vel voventes matrimonium contrahere possunt*, IV, 6.

[8] Cap. unic., *de voto et voti redemptione*, III, 15, in VI°.

[9] Sess. XXIV, *de matrimonio*, c. 9.

fession were invalid, in other words, stating that all religious vows were solemn, it was no longer considered possible that a religious profession could exist and be anything but solemn. From that time on, to be a religious meant also to be bound by solemn vows.[1] Nor was this opinion without foundation. When Boniface VIII declared that the solemnity of religious profession was of ecclesiastical origin, he at the same time declared that those vows only were solemn which were either imposed by the reception of major orders, or which were freely made by either express or tacit religious profession in a Religious Order *approved by the Church.*[2] But already in 1215, the Fourth Lateran Council had decreed that no new order could be founded, and that he who wished to become a religious must select one of the then existing approved Orders.[3] The necessity of papal approbation was later decreed by Gregory X,[4] and by John XXII.[5] Since, therefore, as declared by Boniface VIII, solemn profession existed only in *approved* religious orders, this, when considered in connection with the decrees of the First and Second Lateran Councils, which had declared all marriages contracted by persons bound by religious profession to be invalid, afforded a very firm foundation for holding that, after that time there existed no true religious order in which solemn profession was not made. This opinion becomes more certain because of the fact that Pius V, shortly after the Council of Trent, banned all religious communities in which solemn vows were not made.[6]

Except for particular provisions made by the Holy See for individual cases, solemn profession continued to be the only profession made in approved religious orders, until the latter half

---

[1] "...im Mittelalter war dieselbe (sc. feierliche Profess) mit dem Ordensstande derart verbunden, dass beide Hand in Hand gingen. Wer Ordensmann war, hatte auch feierliche Gelübde abgelegt, und umgekehrt..."—"Feierliche Gelübde und Entstehung des Ordenswesens," *Stimmen aus Maria-Laach*, Erg'bd. XVII, Heft 65, p. 24.

[2] "...illum solum debere dici solemne...quod solemnizatum fuit per susceptionem sacri ordinis, aut per professionem expressam vel tacitam, factam alicui de religionibus per sedem apostolicam approbatis..."—Cap. unic., *de voto et voti redemptione*, III, 15, in VI°.

[3] C. 9, X, *de Religiosis domibus ut episcopo sint subjecti*, III, 36.

[4] Cap. unic., *de religiosis domibus*, III, 17, in VI°.

[5] Cap. unic., *de religiosis domibus*, tit. VII, in Extrav. Joan. XXII.

[6] Const. "*Circa Pastoralis*," May 29, 1566,—*Fontes*, n. 112.

of the nineteenth century. One exception from this legislation was made in favor of the Society of Jesus by Gregory XIII, when he formally approved the constitutions of the Society. Two documents bearing on this matter were issued; the first, "*Quanto Fructuosius*," was issued on February 1, 1583;[1] the other, "*Ascendente Domino*," bears the date of May 25, 1584.[2] In both these documents a concession is granted in virtue of which the novices of the Society, after a period of probation lasting two years, make simple perpetual vows, instead of solemn vows. It is further stated that in spite of the prevalent opinion of the time, the novices by means of these simple vows become religious in the true sense of the word. How strongly and tenaciously the opinion was held, that without solemn profession no one could be considered to be a religious, is shown by these documents.[3] Despite a very clear and evident declaration contained in the first of these documents, there still remained those who could not be convinced of the possibility of a religious not having solemn vows. In order to correct this opinion, Gregory XIII, in the second of the documents, threatened with excommunication, reserved to the Holy See, any one who would presume to deny that the members of the Society, though they made only simple vows, were not true religious.[4]

Another exception from the general legislation concerning solemn profession was made in 1837. On the 24th of March of

---

[1] *Fontes* n. 150.

[2] *Fontes* n. 153.

[3] "...statuimus ac etiam decernimus...omnes...qui in ipsa Societate... tria vota prædicta, tametsi simplicia emiserint emittentque in futurum, vere et proprie Religiosos fuisse, et esse, et ubique et semper, et ab omnibus censeri et nominari debere...; præcipimusque, ne quisquam scrupulum de hoc neutiquam iniicere, neque illud in controversiam, dubium, vel suspicionem ponere audeat quoque modo..."—Const. "*Quanto Fructuosius*," par. 5—*Fontes*, n. 150.

[4] "...Quia tamen non defuit temeraria quorumdam audacia, qui post declarationem, decretum, præceptum, et interdictum nostrum...ausu temerario impugnare, mentemque nostram perverse interpretari non erubescunt, disputantes, et prædicta in dubium revocantes... Præcipimus igitur in virtute S. Obedientiæ, ac sub poenis excommunicationis latæ sententiæ...quarum absolutionem Nobis et Successoribus reservamus, ne quis... dictæ Societatis Institutionum, Constitutiones, vel etiam præsentes...quovis disputandi, vel etiam veritatis indagandæ quæsito colore, directe vel indirecte impugnare vel eis contradicere audeat."—Const. "*Ascendente Domino*"—*Fontes*, n. 153.

that year, permission was granted to all Trappist monasteries within the borders of France, in virtue of which, novices in these communities made only simple profession at the end of the term of probation, instead of the customary solemn vows.[1]

§3 From the Encyclical "Neminem Latet" to the Code 1857—1917

In all approved religious orders, except in those for which the Holy See had granted special concessions, novices continued to make solemn profession immediately after the year of probation, provided they had attained the age of sixteen years, required by the Council of Trent.[2]

On March 19, 1857, Pope Pius IX, through the Congregation in charge of Religious Affairs, issued the Encyclical "*Neminem Latet*"[3], which added a new feature to legislation concerning religious profession. The needs of the times, the letter stated, demanded greater care in admitting candidates to solemn profession, lest such be admitted who are unfit for the religious state.[4] In order to guard against the evils which would result from admitting unworthy candidates, it was decreed that future candidates for each and every order of men[5] of solemn vows, would make simple profession at the completion of the year of probation, provided the age prescribed had been attained.[6] Only after a period of three years in simple vows, were the neo-professed to be admitted to solemn profession. For just and reasonable causes, the proper superiors could defer admission to solemn profession beyond the prescribed three years, but with this provision, that in case of deferment, the solemn profession must be made at or before the time the candidate reaches the age of twenty-five

---

[1] Bizzarri, *Collect.*, pp. 73, 74.

[2] Sess. XXV, *de regularibus*, cap. 15.

[3] Bizzarri, *Collect.*, p. 853 sqq.

[4] "...tristissimis hisce temporibus...maximam adhibendam esse curam solicitudinem, diligentiam, ad eorum spiritum, uti par est, probandam qui vota solemnia Deo nuncupare postulant, ne quis admittatur...sæculi contagione pollutus..."—Encycl. "*Neminem Latet*," Bizzarri, *Collect.*, pp. 853–854.

[5] Decr. S. C. Ep. et Reg., 19 Mart. 1857—*Fontes*, n. 1976.

[6] "Peracta probatione et novitiatu...novitii vota simplicia emittant." Encycl. "*Neminem Latet*," par. 3, *loc. cit.*

years.[1] But if the candidate, at the completion of the novitiate year had already attained the age of twenty-five years, he had, nevertheless, to spend the required three years in simple vows before being admitted to solemn profession.[2] But under the same circumstances of age, the superior was not permitted to defer solemn profession beyond the three-year period[3] unless special permission for each case had been obtained from the Congregation in charge of Religious Affairs.[4]

The nature of the simple vows required by the Encyclical "*Neminem Latet*" was further explained in the decree "*Sanctissimus*," issued by the Congregation of Bishops and Regulars on June 12, 1858. This decree declared that the vows were perpetual on the part of the candidate;[5] the power of dispensing from them was reserved to the Holy See;[6] but should the neo-professed, for any reason whatsoever, prove himself unfit for the religious state, the order was fully empowered to dismiss such an unworthy religious at any time during the duration of his simple vows. In the event of such a dismissal, the religious, by that very fact, was released from his vows, and freed from all obligations contracted by his profession.[7] By his simple profession, the candidate was truly incorporated into the order and enjoyed all the privileges of the solemnly professed members.[8] The simply professed religious did not, however, give up the ownership of his

---

[1] "Professi post triennium a die quo vota simplicia emiserint...ad professionem votorum solemnium admittantur...Poterit...superior ex justis et rationabilibus causis, differre, non tamen ultra ætatem annorum 25 expletorum." Encycl. "*Neminem Latet*," par. 4, *loco cit.*

[2] S. C. Ep. et Reg., Aug. 16, 1866—Bizzarri, *Collect.*, p. 858, 859.

[3] "In cong. propositum fuit dubium a P. D. Bonifacio Wimmer Abbate Præs. Cassinensium in America exhibitum; Quod adhuc dubitatur utrum in casu quo sacerdos habitum petivit et obtinuit, qui annum 25 longe transgressus est huic (emissa professione v. simplicium) professio solemnis...differri posse supra consuetum triennium si...intra triennium (votorum simplicium) non sufficientia argumenta de sua vocatione dederit?" "Em. Patres rescripserunt negative (nempe non posse differri)"—S. C. Ep. et Reg. resp. ad dubium 16 Aug., 1866—Bizzarri, *Collect.*, p. 867.

[4] Note in Bizzarri, *Collect.*, p. 867.

[5] N. I, Bizzarri, *Collect.*, p. 855.

[6] *Ibid.*, n. II.

[7] *Ibid.*, n. III.

[8] *Ibid.*, n. VI.

property but, in virtue of his simple vow of poverty, relinquished simply the free and independent use and administration of such property.[1]

Pius IX, on February 7, 1862, issued the constitution "*Ad Universalis*," which contained important new legislation concerning the simple vows prescribed by the encyclical "*Neminem Latet*." Cases were brought to the knowledge of the Holy See, in which novices, contrary to the decrees of the encyclical, had been advanced to solemn profession immediately after their novitiate. Doubts arose in the minds of the superiors concerning the validity of such solemn professions. To remove all doubts, Pius IX, in the Constitution, "*Ad Universalis*," ordained that for the future no solemn profession would be valid unless it had been preceded by the period of simple profession prescribed by the Encyclical "*Neminem Latet*."[2]

Although the Constitution "*Ad Universalis*" provided against any future doubt, it made no declaration in reference to the validity or invalidity of professions made contrary to the Encyclical "*Neminem Latet*," but before the Constitution, "*Ad Universalis*" had been issued. The Congregation of Bishops and Regulars, on August 16, 1866, declared that the solemn profession in these cases had been made validly, but illicitly.[3]

The prescriptions of the Encyclical "*Neminem Latet*" and of the decree "*Ad Universalis*" applied only to orders of men. For religious orders of women, the former discipline remained in force, in consequence of which, solemn profession for them continued to be the only profession made immediately after the novitiate, except where the Holy See had made special provisions for individual cases. Such a provision had been made for the convents of France.[4] Another such provision is recorded in favor of a certain convent in which, because of the interference of civil

[1] *Ibid.*, n. IX.

[2] "...statuimus ac decernimus nullam omnio, irritam et nullius roboris fore professionem votorum sollemnium tam scienter, quam ignoranter, quovis modo, prætextu, et colore factam a novitiis quibuscumque etiam laicis, et conversis, qui licet probationem, et novitiatum prout de jure expleverint, non emittant prius professionem votorum simplicium, et in ea per triennium non permanserint..." Decr. "*Ad Universalis*"—*Fontes*, n. 532.

[3] Bizzarri, *Collect.*, p. 867.

[4] Bizzarri, *Collect.*, p. 736.

legislation, solemn vows could not be made immediately after the novitiate.[1] A letter of the Congregation of Bishops and Regulars, of March 19, 1857, authorized the bishops of Austria to grant permission to communities of nuns in their jurisdiction in virtue of which novices could make simple vows before assuming the obligations of solemn profession.[2] On September 30, 1864, a letter was addressed to the Archbishop of Baltimore by the Congregation of Bishops and Regulars,[3] in which letter several provisions were made in reference to the Sisterhoods of the United States. Vows, which up to the date of the letter, had been made by the Nuns of the Visitation, B.V.M., in Georgetown, Mobile, Kaskaskia, St. Louis and Baltimore, were declared to be solemn. But due to the circumstances of the times, it was further stated that all novices in the future, making profession for the Convents above enumerated, were to make simple vows, and after having spent five years in simple profession, they could be admitted to solemn profession. In reference to other communities not above enumerated, the Congregation, in the same letter, declared that unless a special rescript had been obtained from the Holy See, novices could make only simple profession. It was finally stipulated that candidates for any convent which would be established in any of the States after the date of the letter, would be permitted to make only simple vows.

A decree, issued May 3, 1902, brought a change in the legislation pertaining to profession of religious women. By the decree "*Perpensis*,"[4] issued on that date by the Congregation of Bishops and Regulars, the prescriptions of the Encyclical "*Neminem Latet*," of March 19, 1857, and of the decree "*Ad Universalis*," of February 7, 1862, were extended to all orders of women making solemn vows. In virtue of this decree, all novices of orders of women of solemn vows, were, at the end of the novitiate, to make simple vows; after spending three years in simple vows they could be admitted to solemn profession. If a particular community had received an indult permitting that a longer period of time elapse between simple and solemn profession, the indult was not cancelled by the decree "*Perpensis*."

---

[1] S. C. Ep. et Reg. 21 April 1841—Bizzarri, *Collect.*, pp. 463, 464.

[2] Bizzarri, *Collect.*, pp. 736, 737.

[3] *Fontes*, n. 1995.

[4] *ASS*, XXXV (1902-1903), 31sq.

Moreover, if circumstances warranted, Ordinaries or Superior-generals could, in a particular case, grant permission to extend the period of simple profession beyond the required three years, with the limitation, however, that it could not be extended beyond the time the candidate attained the age of twenty-five years. The simple vows prescribed by the decree were perpetual; dispensation from them was reserved to the Holy See. During the time spent in simple profession the religious retained ownership of property, but the administration of such property rested with the superior.

The prescriptions of the Encyclical "*Neminem Latet*" and "*Ad Universalis*," concerning profession in orders of men, and those of the decree "*Perpensis*," bearing on the profession of nuns, remained in force until the promulgation of the Code. The promulgation of the Code brought another important change in this matter; instead of demanding simple perpetual vows before solemn profession, the Code now requires simple triennial vows only.[1]

Article 3

CONGREGATIONS OF SIMPLE VOWS BEFORE THE CODE

A religious congregation may be defined as a legitimately approved religious society, whose members make public, but simple vows, either temporary or perpetual in their duration, according to the constitution of the individual society.[2] The chief characteristic distinction of the congregation is, that its members do not make solemn, but only simple, vows.

It has already been seen from the history of solemn profession that for several centuries the existence of such congregations was well nigh impossible. The First Lateran Council in 1123,[3] and the Second Lateran Council in 1139,[4] by decreeing marriages contracted by persons who had made religious profession, to be null and void, implicitly declared all religious vows to be solemn. In 1215, the Fourth Lateran Council forbade the

1 Can. 574.

2 Can. 488, 1°, 2°.

3 C. 21—*Mansi*, XXI, 286.

4 Cc. 17, 18—*Mansi*, XXI, 527–528.

founding of new religious orders by decreeing that any one who wished to become a religious, had to do so by making profession in one of the approved orders.[1] Similar decrees were later issued by Pope Gregory X,[2] and by Pope John XXII.[3] The purpose of this legislation was to forestall the formation of too great a variety of religious orders.

In the sixteenth century,[4] however, contrary to the legislation just cited, there arose communities who made only simple vows. These were formed without any approbation on the part of the Holy See; some of them, it seems, had received episcopal sanction.[5] Against these communities, Pope Pius V issued his Constitution "*Circa Pastoralis*," on the 29th of May, 1566.[6] In this constitution, he commanded all the members of such societies to make solemn vows, and to observe the papal enclosure under threat of severe punishment.[7] If they failed to comply with the commands contained in the constitution, they were forbidden to receive new candidates; if despite this regulation, they nevertheless continued to receive new members, it was declared that the professions of such candidates would be null and void.[8] On November 17, 1568, through his constitution "*Lubricum vitæ genus*,"[9] Pope Pius V issued a second condemnation against societies making only simple vows. He commanded that within twenty-four hours after receiving notice of the constitution, they must adopt one of the approved rules, and within one month make solemn vows.

Despite the stringent measures of Pope Pius V, societies of simple vows were never entirely abolished. Though canonically non-existent, many of them continued to function and to receive new members.[10] Subsequent Popes did not issue any distinct decrees against them; some, however, did express a desire that

---

1 C. 9, X, *de Religiosis domibus, ut Episcopis sint subjectæ*, III, 36.

2 Cap. unic., *de Religiosis domibus*, III, 17, in VI°.

3 Cap. unic., *de Religiosis domibus*, tit. VII, in Extrav. Joan. XXII.

4 Vicente, *Recentia Instituta*, cap. I, n. 1; Sipos, *Enchiridion J. C.*, p. 316.

5 Vicente, *loc. cit.*

6 *Fontes*, n. 112.

7 §III.

8 §IV, §VI.

9 *Bull. Rom.*, VII, 725–726.

10 Schaaf, *The Cloister*, p. 54; Turner, *The Vow of Poverty*, pp. 45–46; Vicente, *Recentia Instituta*, cap. I, n. 3.

the legislation enacted by Pius V should be strictly observed.[1] In the course of time, however, the Holy See began to tolerate these communities, and gradually, toleration gave way to positive approbation.[2]

Benedict XIII, in his Bulla "*Pretiosa*," of May 25, 1727,[3] stated that he had no desire of prohibiting such foundations. A few years later, Clement XII nullified the bull "*Pretiosa*" of Benedict XIII.[4] But Benedict XIV was more kindly disposed toward these Institutes without, however, giving them formal approbation. Speaking in particular of the Institute of Mary, or English Ladies, he stated that they should be tolerated, though not approved by the Holy See.[5] The care of these he entrusted to the local Ordinaries, who were advised to treat the institutes with kindness.[6]

As the years went by, when it became more and more evident what a source for good these societies could be, the Holy See was wont to be more favorably disposed toward them. It was not, however, until 1900, that any general legislation was promulgated concerning them. On December 8 of that year, Pope Leo XIII issued the Constitution "*Conditæ a Christo*,"[7] which Vicente calls the "*Magna Charter*" for Institutes of simple vows.[8]

In the very beginning of the Constitution, Leo XIII divided these Institutes into two classes—those of diocesan right, that had received only episcopal approbation, and those of Pontifical right, whose approbation had come directly from the Holy See.[9]

A point, worthy of note, concerning the institutes is the fact that before the Code, their members were not considered *religious*.[10]

---

[1] Turner, *The Vow of Poverty*, pp. 75–76.

[2] Vicente, *Recentia Instituta, loc. cit.*

[3] *Bull. Rom.*, XXII, 542.

[4] Bulla "*Romanus Pontifex*," 30 Mart. 1737, *Bull. Rom.*, XXIII, 324.

[5] "...Dictarum vero virginum conservatoria, licet ab Apostolica Sede... non approbata, ab hac tamen benigne tolerari..."—Const. "*Quamvis Justo*," 30 Apr. 1749, XIII,—*Fontes*, n. 398.

[6] §XXIII of the same Constitution.

[7] *Fontes*, n. 644.

[8] *Recentia Instituta*, cap. I, n. 4.

[9] "Duplex...earundem est ratio; aliæ quæ Episcoporum solummodo approbationem nactæ ob eam rem *diœcesanæ* appellantur; aliæ vero de quibus præterea Pontificis sententiæ intercessit..."

[10] Piat. *Prælectiones Juris Regularis*, I, 7–10; Sipos, *Enchiridion, J. C.*, p. 315–316.

In canonical language they were called, not *religiosi*, but *sodales;* and the institutes were termed *sodalitates piæ*. This fact is borne out by various pronouncements of the Holy See. Thus, for instance, Benedict XIV, in his Constitution "*Quamvis Justo*," stated that the Institute of Mary, or English Ladies, concerning whom the Constitution treats in particular, were not true religious.[1] The Congregation of Bishops and Regulars expressed itself in like manner on several occasions. When asked whether the Redemptorists could be called religious, in the canonical interpretation of the word, the Congregation gave a negative response on September 16, 1864.[2] Although generally speaking, members of Institutes of simple vows were not considered religious, some such societies were granted privileges in this matter. Thus, for instance, the Jesuits' vows were declared to be only simple vows by Pope Gregory XIII,[3] but he nevertheless emphatically stated that despite their simple vows, they were truly religious.[4]

A new regulation was brought into effect with the promulgation of the Code. Since 1918, all persons making the vows in an approved community are truly religious, without any distinction as to whether the society for which the vows are made is one in which solemn or only simple vows are made.[5]

Article 4

PERPETUAL AND TEMPORARY PROFESSION BEFORE THE CODE

The religious state, of its very nature, requires a certain stability, perseverance of its members. Mindful of the words of Christ: "No man putting his hand to the plough, and looking back, is fit for the kingdom of God,"[6] the Fathers of religious life, from its very beginning, emphasized the necessity of perseverance.

---

1 §13.

2 *Fontes*, n. 1993.

3 Const. "*Quantum Fructuosius*"—*Fontes*, n. 150; Const. "*Ascendente Domino*,"—*Fontes*, n. 153.

4 *Ibid.*

5 Cf. can. 488.

6 *Luke*, IX, 62.

St. Cyprian urged the virgins not to forsake the state of virginity they had embraced;[1] he asked them to persevere, living the life of chastity they had promised, and thus bravely and firmly to await the reward of their virginity.[2]

Perseverance of its members in religious life was likewise insisted upon from the earliest periods of monasticism. Schenute considered it an act of denial and betrayal for one to leave the monastic precincts after having promised to lead a life consecrated to God.[3] So also St. Benedict, in his rule, prescribes perpetual profession. When speaking of the admission of novices, he says that once they have made profession they may no longer leave the monastic community, nor wrest their necks from under the yoke of the rule.[4] St. Cæsarius, a contemporary of St. Benedict, in the first chapter of his rule, says that, only on condition that they persevere until death, should candidates for the community be received.[5]

Ecclesiastical legislation on this point gives many evidences of the perpetuity of religious profession in the early fourth and fifth century decrees of synods and councils, as well as instructions issued by the Supreme Pontiffs. In proof of this it is necessary only to refer to the decrees and canons of councils, already quoted in a foregoing article of this treatise, bearing on the contracting of marriage after profession.[6] But aside from the decrees already cited, there are many others which, without reference to marriage, prohibit the return of religious to secular life. The Council of Chalcedon (451) declared that no one who had entered a monastic community was afterwards to be permitted to enter military service, or to receive secular distinctions.[7] The Council of Arles (452) threatened with severe punishment any religious who would forsake his chosen life.[8] The Council of

---

[1] "...servate virgines, servate quod esse coepistis, servate quod eritis..." —*De habit. virg.*, c. 22—*MPL*, IV, 461.

[2] *Ep. 62 ad Pomponium*, c.;2—*MPL*. IV, 366.

[3] Leipoldt, *Schenute von Atripe*, p. 110; cf. also Piontek, *De Indulto Exclaustrationis necnon Sæcularizationis*, pp. 21-22.

[4] *Reg. S. P. N. Benedicti*, cap. 58.

[5] *MPL*, LXVII, 1099; Chapman, *St. Benedict and the Sixth Century*, p. 122.

[6] Cf. Art. 2, §1, of the present chapter.

[7] C. 27—*Mansi*, VII, 395.

[8] C. 25—*Mansi*, VII, 881.

Paris (615) forbade, under pain of excommunication *usque ad exitum vitæ*, a religious to abandon the life of the monastery.[1] The sixth Council of Toledo (638) declared that return to the secular life was unlawful for anyone who had accepted the religious habit.[2] Pope Eugene II, in 826, issued a similar instruction,[3] as did later on, Pope Nicholas I (858–867).[4] The Council of Worms, (868), in its twenty-first canon, decreed that severe punishment would be inflicted upon the religious who would presume to take up secular life in the world.[5] The First Lateran Council, in 1123,[6] and the Second Lateran Council, in 1139,[7] declared all marriages null and void in which one of the contracting parties was bound by religious. profession. This declaration determined that all future professions were solemn. Solemn profession is, of its very nature, perpetual, so that from that time on, there could be no longer question of any but perpetual profession.

In March, 1857, Pope Pius IX, in the Encyclical "*Neminem Latet*," demanded that simple profession precede the making of solemn vows.[8] This new legislation did not, however, effect a change in the perpetuity of profession. A subsequent decree, "*Sanctissimus*," in 1858, expressly stated that this simple profession was perpetual on the part of the candidate.[9] A similar declaration was made in reference to the simple profession of nuns demanded by the decree "*Perpensis*," of May 3, 1902.[10] Temporary profession was practically unknown before the promulgation of the Code.[11] There are, however, on record, instances where the Holy See granted permission in particular cases for temporary profession. Such a permission was granted to the

---

[1] C. 14—*Hefele*, III, 69.
[2] C. 6—*Hefele*, III, 90.
[3] C. 31, C. XXVII, q. 1.
[4] *Mansi*, XV, 443.
[5] *Mansi*, XV, 873.
[6] C. 8, D. XXVII.
[7] C. 40, C. XXVII, q. 1.
[8] Bizzarri, *Collect.*, 853–854.
[9] N. I, Bizzarri, *Collect.*, p. 855.
[10] *ASS*, XXXV (1902–1903), 31 sqq.
[11] Vicente, *Recentia Instituta*, tract. II, cap. V, n. 200; Goyeneche, "De Transitu ad aliam Religionem," *CpR*, I (1920), 110; Larraona, *CpR*, II, (1921), 208–209.

Vincentian Sisters of Charity of Szathmar in Hungary. In virtue of a brief of September 15, 1835, these sisters were permitted to make their profession with the proviso "as long as I remain in the community."[1] Another such particular permission was granted in favor of the Lay Brothers of the American Cassinese Congregation of Benedictines. According to the *Declarations* of this Congregation, which were approved in 1908, the Lay Brothers made triennial profession before being admitted to perpetual profession.[2] Although these declarations were finally approved only in 1908, the prescriptions therein contained had been sanctioned *per modum experimenti* since 1898.[3]

---

[1] Cf. *AkKR*, 72 (1894), 518.

[2] Cf. *Declarationes in Regulam S. P. N. Benedicti et Statuta Congregationis Americano-Cassinensis*, c. 58, *declaratio III*. (Typis Archiabbatiæ S. Vincentii, A.D. 1909).

[3] Cf. Decree of S. C. de Prop. Fide, *op. cit.*, p. ii.

APPENDIX

ROMAN LAW AND RELIGIOUS PROFESSION

Very little concerning the subject of the Act of Religious Profession may be found in Roman Law sources. Monks and Monastic life were not, however, entirely unknown to the law of the Empire. Legislation having some reference to religious profession may be reduced to two main heads, namely, the admission into the religious state, and the perpetuity of profession.

Concerning the first point, the Novels require that when a person presents himself for admission into a monastic community, the superior must first make a diligent investigation into the character of the applicant. If there be nothing against the person, he may be admitted. But if the person is entirely unknown, he may not be permitted to make his profession until after a period of three years. If during this period, no accusations of any kind are brought to the knowledge of the superior, the applicant may then be received.[1] By far the greater part of Justinian's legislation concerning the admission had to do with slaves. Slaves were under the absolute dominium of their owners.[2] In consequence they could not become religious without the knowledge and permission of their masters. Once they had received this permission, they were free to become religious.[3] A slave who, with the full knowledge of his master, made religious profession, enjoyed thereafter the rights of a free person, but under the condition that he would persevere in the religious life. Just as soon as he left the monastery he lost his liberty, and again became the property of his former master.[4] On the other hand, a slave who, without the knowledge of his master, applied for

---

[1] *Nov.* 123, 35.
[2] *I*, 1, 8, 1.
[3] *Cod.* I, 3, 37 (38).
[4] *Cod.* I, 3, 37 (38).

admission into a monastic community, could not be permitted to make his profession. If the master of the slave was known, the slave had to be returned to him. But if the master was not known, the applicant was not permitted to make profession immediately. It was necessary that a period of three years elapse after his application. If during this period the master of the slave became known and laid claim to his property, the slave was obliged to return. But if during the three years no one claimed the slave, he could then be permitted to make his profession.[1]

Concerning the perpetuity of profession, Roman Law legislated that no monk could be permitted to leave the monastic life, once he had made his profession. If he presumed to do otherwise, he was subjected to corporal punishment and a fine, unless within one year he would return to his monastery.[2] Later on it was declared that monks who forsake monastic life would forfeit their possessions.[3] In the Novels it is stated that a religious who does not persevere in the life he has chosen, must himself give an account to God of his conduct; when he leaves the monastery the possessions he owned at the time of his entrance do not revert to him, but remain the property of the monastery.[4] If a fugitive monk attempted to enter upon a secular career, the bishop, or the ruler of the province was obliged to deprive the monk of his position, and compel him to return to his monastery. If after that, he would dare to leave again, he, by that very fact, became a servant of the governor.[5]

---

[1] *Nov.* 123, 35.
[2] *Cod.* I, 3, 52, 9.
[3] *Cod.* I, 3, 54, 7.
[4] *Nov.* 5, 4–6.
[5] *Nov.* 123, 42.

PART II

PRESENT LEGISLATION

CHAPTER IV

NECESSARY QUALIFICATIONS OF CANDIDATES

Religious profession may be called the gateway or portal to religious life—the life of those who, in an especial manner, devote their efforts to striving after perfection, by the observance of the Evangelical Counsels of obedience, chastity and poverty. Not any and every person is qualified for this kind of life. Hence it will be necessary, in the first place, to ascertain the qualifications which every person who aspires to religious life must possess. For the sake of clearness, these qualifications may be divided into two general classes, namely, into *positive* and *negative* qualifications.

Article 1

POSITIVE QUALIFICATIONS

Canon 538 of the Code in a general way points out the qualifications an aspirant to the religious state must have:

In religionem admitti potest quilibet Catholicus qui nullo legitimo detineatur impedimento rectaque intentione moveatur, et ad religionis onera ferenda sit idoneus.

According to this canon, four qualifications are required in the aspirant. 1. He must be a member of the Catholic Church. 2. He must be free from impediments to religious life. 3. He must be actuated by a proper motive for wishing to become a religious. 4. He must be capable of bearing the burdens of this kind of life, and be fit to carry on the work which may be assigned to him. In the present article only three points will be considered: the requisite of true religion, the intention, and the general fitness of the candidate. A consideration of the impediments to religious life will be left for the second article of this chapter.

§1 Catholicity

The first and primary qualification which the Code demands of every aspirant to the religious state is that he be a Catholic at the time of his admission, that is, he must actually be a member of the Catholic Church.[1] "Since no religious institute," Augustine says, "can legally exist without the approval of the Church, and the Church in concrete terms is the Catholic Church, it is evident that the religious state is open only to such as acknowledge the legitimate authority of that Church."[2]

In describing the religious state, the Code says that it is a permanent mode of life, in which the *faithful* by means of the vows of obedience, chastity, and poverty undertake to practise the Evangelical Counsels.[3] Emphasis must be put on the fact that it is the *faithful* (*fideles*), who make up the personnel of the religious state. But no one can be numbered among the faithful, or called *fideles*, unless he be a member of the Church of Christ and be in actual communion with her. Membership in the Church of Christ is obtained by baptism.[4] Hence any person who has not received baptism is not a member of the Church of Christ, and in consequence may not be admitted to the religious state. Under this class of persons, who because of this lack of baptism are excluded from the religious life, must be numbered all infidels and pagans, such as the Jews, the Turks, and the Mohammedans.[5] Catechumens must also be excluded from the religious state. Although receiving instructions preparatory to their being received into the Church, they are as yet, not members[6] in the canonical interpretation of the word, because they lack initiation by baptism. Before their reception of baptism, they cannot be called "Catholics," nor can they be numbered among the "faithful," as understood in canons 487 and 538 and, therefore they are deficient in that first and fundamental qualification, that condition *sine qua non*, for admission into the religious state.[7]

---

[1] Papi, *Religious in Church Law*, p. 5.

[2] *Commentary*, III, 198; cf. also Papi, *Religious in Church Law*, p. 5.

[3] Can. 487.

[4] "Baptismate homo constituitur in Ecclesia Christi persona..." can. 87; "...per baptisma veluti per januam ingreditur homo in hanc domum Patrisfamilias quæ est ecclesia..."—Maroto, *Institutiones*, n. 391.

[5] Fanfani, *De Jure Religiosorum*, p. 197; Bakalarcyzk, *De Novitiatu*, p. 55.

[6] Maroto, *Institutiones*, n. 391.

[7] Fanfani, *op. cit.*, p. 198; Pejska, *Jus Canonicum Religiosorum*, p. 78.

Canon 487, as already indicated, states that the members of the religious orders and congregations are taken from among the faithful or *fideles*. This leads to the conclusion that such persons who are not faithful to the Church whose members they are because of baptism, in other words, those persons who, though they have been baptized, do not live in communion with the Church, are likewise to be denied admission to religious life. The reason for this is that they do not possess in its fullest degree the *Catholicitas* demanded by canon 538. Hence heretics, schismatics, and all non-catholics in general, while living in heresy or schism; apostates before their return to the Church must, like the unbaptized infidels and pagans, be refused entrance to religious life.[1]

There remains yet another class of persons who must be considered here—the excommunicated. May such persons be granted admittance to a religious order or congregation? Excommunication is a censure by which a baptized person is excluded from the body of the faithful.[2] It goes without saying that excommunication cannot remove the indelible character imprinted upon the soul by baptism; but it does exclude the censured person from communion with the faithful so that he can no longer be called "*fidelis*." Some theologians in fact, assert that, excepting only the baptismal character, the excommunicated person ceases to be a member of the Church.[3]

A synod held in Paris about the year 1212, declared that if a person who had been excommunicated, or who had fallen under the personal interdict, wishes to become a religious, he must first reveal this condition of his to the monastic superior so that the necessary dispensation may be obtained.[4] From this, one may infer that the synod in question considered such persons ineligible for the religious state. Billuart is of the opinion that excommunicated persons, even though they be *tolerati*, may not licitly be received into a religious order or congregation because, he

[1] Pejska, *Jus Canonicum Religiosorum*, p. 78; Schaefer, *De Religiosis*, p. 254; Bakalarczyk, *De Novitiatu*, pp. 54, 55; Pruemmer, *Manuale J. C.*, q. 199; Vermeersch-Creusen, *Epitome*, I, 385; Augustine, *Commentary*, I, 198.

[2] Can. 2257 §I; Chelodi, *Jus Poenale*, p. 44; Hyland, *Excommunication*, p. 1.

[3] For a further discussion of this point cf. Hyland, *Excommunication*, pp. 7 sqq.

[4] C. 15—*Mansi*, XXII, 830.

says, such persons may not enter into communication with the faithful.[1]

To admit into a religious community one who is under the censure of excommunication would be to frustrate the fundamental aim and purpose of this ecclesiastical penalty. The purpose of every excommunication is to bring back to a sense of duty the erring person[2] by barring him from communication with the rest of the faithful. This idea of separation would be entirely lost if such a person were permitted to become a member of a religious community, the aim and end of which must of necessity unite its members into one large family. Hence it would seem that it is illicit to receive an excommunicated person into a religious community before absolution from the censure has been received.

§2 Intention

Just as in other acts, so also in embracing the religious state, the candidate must be actuated by a proper motive or intention. To renounce the world and to dedicate oneself to God in religious life is an act above the ordinary, material affairs of every day life; it is a spiritual, a supernatural act. In order to be honest with himself, and to receive the graces attached to this abnegation of self, the candidate must put aside all worldly motives of gain, and act with a purely supernatural intention.[3]

In order that a candidate have the proper intention for embracing the religious state, he must be actuated by motives which go hand in hand with the ultimate end of the religious state.[4] The fundamental idea of the religious state was enunciated by our Divine Master Himself when He said: "If thou wilt be perfect, go sell what thou hast...and come follow me."[5] The underlying principle of the religious state is the striving after perfection by living in close union with Christ. The religious state,

[1] "...Excommunicatus, etiamsi toleratus, illicite recipitur in religione... ille...non potest se ingerere communicationi fidelium; unde et ipse peccat, et qui ipsum recipit..." *Cursus Theologiæ*, tom IV, tract. de S. Rel., Diss. IV, art. 1.

[2] Hyland, *Excommunication*, p. 1.

[3] Jansen, *Ordensrecht*, p. 92.

[4] Papi, *Religious in Church Law*, p. 5; Schaefer, *De Religiosis*, p. 254; Pruemmer, *Manuale J. C.*, q. 199.

[5] *Matt.* XIX, 21.

therefore, is a state in which perfection is to be sought after,[1] or in a word, it is the state of perfection to be acquired.[2] The primary motive, therefore, of every aspirant to this state must be to strive after perfection and thus to accomplish the salvation of his immortal soul.[3] But, as Papi rightly asserts, "this intention does not need to be absolutely explicit. Anyone who wishes to follow Christ more closely, or to be able to work for the glory of God, and the salvation of souls at the sacrifice of his own comforts, does not lack the necessary right intention."[4]

While the primary motive for entering religion must be the attainment of perfection, this does not exclude secondary motives, provided only that they be compatible with the primary motive. It is a dictate of sound philosophy that in striving after the primary end, a person may at the same time occupy himself with such secondary ends which will assist him in the acquisition of the final and primary one. Hence it is not in the least incongruous that in embracing the religious state, the candidate be actuated also by such secondary motives as the pursuance of literary culture, missionary work, the care of souls, or of the sick and infirm.[5]

To enter religion out of any material or worldly motive, would be gravely sinful. If a person were to embrace the religious state actuated only by motives which are far from supernatural, he would place himself in great danger of becoming unfaithful to the life he proposes to lead. Hence to enter the religious state for the purpose of attaining dignities, or out of human respect, or out of purely material interests, would be gravely sinful and illicit, because such motives are directly opposed to the *recta intentio* demanded by canon 538.[6] The Church has at various times explicitly condemned such improper worldly motives. Pope Alexander II, in 1603, declared that no one may receive the monastic habit with the hope of his becoming an abbot.[7]

[1] Can. 593; Pruemmer, *Manuale J. C.*, q. 199.

[2] St. Thomas, 2*a*, 2*æ*, q. 186, a. 2 ad 1.

[3] Fanfani, *De Jure Religiosorum*, p. 203; Augustine, *Commentary*, III, 199; Sipos, *Enchiridion J. C.*, p. 343.

[4] *Religious in Church Law*, p. 5.

[5] Sipos, *Enchiridion J. C.*, p. 343; Pruemmer, *Manuale J. C.*, q. 199; Schaefer, *De Religiosis*, p. 254.

[6] Pruemmer, *Manuale J. C.*, q. 199; Fanfani, *De Jure Religiosorum*, p. 203.

[7] C. 20, C. XVI, q. 7.

Pope Sixtus V, in his constitution "*Cum de omnibus,*" of November 26, 1587, forbade the reception of persons guilty of divers crimes because, he said, such persons desire to become religious not out of any pious intention, but in order to escape the just punishment for their crimes.[1]

Other motives may be good in themselves, but because they are incompatible or not in keeping with the primary motive which must actuate the aspirant, they cannot be said to be proper motives for embracing religious life, and in consequence would likewise be opposed to the prescriptions of canon 538, with the result that candidates actuated by such motives may not licitly be granted admission. Such motives would be, for example, if one would enter a religious community solely because of a friendship he has with a person already a member of that community; or again, if a person would be under a wrong impression that the life of a religious is one of ease and comfort, and under the influence of such false impressions, would embrace religious life for the purpose of escaping a life of care and trouble in the world.[2]

It is the duty and obligation of every religious superior in whom rests the admission of candidates, to inquire diligently into the true motive of every one who applies for admittance into the community. If he fails in this duty, he is exposing himself to the danger of admitting candidates who are in no way fitted for the life in the monastery or convent—a thing which may cause great detriment both to the community and to the individual in question. In this connection, it will be well to bear in mind the direction of Pope Clement VIII:

> **Superiores diligenter exquirunt, quo spiritu, qua mente, ac voluntate id regularis vitæ genus elegerint, quem sibi finem proposuerint, num zelo melioris frugis, ac perfectioris vitæ, et ut Deo liberius famulari possint, an potius levitate, vel humano aliquo affectu, aut inordinato animi motu ducantur....**[3]

---

1 "...non pia intentione, sed ad evitandam legum et judiciorum severitatem, quia tuto in sæculo vivere non possunt, tunc demum quærunt a religione auxilium, quando aliunde non sperant...", IV—*Fontes*, n. 162.

2 Papi, *Religious in Church Law*, p. 5.

3 Const. "*Cum ad Regularem,*" 19 Mart. 1603, §5—*Fontes*, n. 189; cf. also Micheletti, *Jus Pianum*, p. 512.

§3 Fitness for Religious Life

A third qualification which canon 538 demands for admittance to religious life, is that the candidate be capable of bearing the burdens of the life to which he aspires. This fitness will be general and particular[1] in so far as it is considered from the viewpoint of religious life in general, or in reference to the requirements of some particular religious order or congregation.

Religious life in general demands a sound mind, a sound body, and a strong character, a character capable of adapting itself to religious discipline. It would be difficult to lay down strict, iron-clad rules according to which a candidate's fitness or unfitness could be judged. Superiors, with the aid of their counselors or chapters, must decide in each individual case. It will not, however, be out of place to recount the more evident defects which authorities in general deem sufficient ground for refusing to accept a given candidate. Among other defects, authors in the first place mention insanity.[2] Serious bodily ills and deformities likewise constitute a sufficient cause for judging a candidate unfit. Among these bodily defects, must be enumerated blindness, deafness, and such deformities which would expose the religious to derision.[3] A candidate, whose health is so impaired as to render it difficult for him to live the life of a religious, must also be refused admission.[4] Fanfani considers also the following to be undesirable candidates: persons who, on account of a natural innate dullness (*hebetudo*), are by their very nature incapable of attaining to religious perfection; persons afflicted with certain uncontrollable vices, such as intense anger, habitual drunkenness, or extreme fickleness of character, when there is little or no hope that time and effort will eradicate these deficiencies.[5] Mothon would exclude also persons who give evidence of possessing a habitual, violent, or passionate disposition, or who suffer from unconquerable jealousy, or spells of melancholy.[6]

---

[1] Augustine, *Commentary*, III, 200.
[2] Papi; *Religious in Church Law*, p. 6.
[3] Fanfani, *De Jure Religiosorum*, p. 204.
[4] Jansen, *Ordensrecht*, p. 92; Mothon, *Institutions Canoniques*, I, 593.
[5] *De Jure Religiosorum*, pp. 203–204.
[6] *Institutions Canoniques*, I, 595.

As far as particular fitness is concerned, it will be necessary to judge this from a consideration of the particular work or aim of each religious order or congregation. Some orders devote themselves mainly to teaching, others to missionary endeavors. Others again may be occupied in hospital or social activities, in the care of the sick and the destitute. In order efficiently to accomplish these various aims, a particular aptitude will be necessary; if this is lacking in the candidate who asks to be received, he must naturally be refused.

In deciding whether or not a candidate is fitted for the life he aspires to embrace, religious superiors and those with whom the acceptance or refusal of applicants rests, must ever be mindful of the fact that the religious state is a state in which perfection is to be *sought after.* Hence canon 538 does not demand that, in granting admission to a candidate, he possess the required qualifications in their highest degree. Otherwise there would hardly be need of a year of novitiate. During this period of probation, many of these requirements can be cultivated and developed. In this connection, it will be well to call to mind the direction given by Pope Alexander VII, when he says that candidates may not be denied admission without a reasonable cause.[1]

Article 2

IMPEDIMENTS

Besides the positive qualifications, treated of in the preceding article, canon 538 demands further that the candidate for religious life be free from all impediments. These impediments are enumerated in canon 542 of the Code. It is true that this canon refers directly to the novitiate, but since the novitiate is but a preparation for profession, canon 542 has at least indirect bearing on profession. Hence it will not be entirely out of place in this treatise on profession to give a brief explanation of these impediments.

---

[1] "Neophytos Deo sub religionis jugo servire volentes sine rationabili causa regulares non respuant, sed pari charitate omnes, qui spiritu Dei aguntur, et ad perfectionem anhelant, amplectantur."—Const. "*Sacrosancti*," 18 Jan. 1658, II, 6—*Fontes*, n. 235.

Impediments to the religious state are either diriment or impedient. The former forbid the candidate's reception and subsequent novitiate under pain of nullity, while the latter will not cause the reception and novitiate to be invalid, but only illicit.

§1 Diriment Impediments

a) *Qui sectæ acatholicæ adhæserunt*

No one who has belonged to a non-catholic sect may validly be admitted to the novitiate. For some time the true interpretation of this law remained obscure, so that it was applied to every person who had at any time been a member of some non-catholic religious body.[1] The Commission for the interpretation of the Code clarified the situation on October 16, 1919, by giving response to the following question:

Utrum verba 'Qui sectæ acatholicæ adhæserunt', canonis 542 sint intelligenda de iis, qui Dei gratia moti ex hæresi vel schismate, in quibus nati sunt, ad Ecclesiam pervenerint; an potius de iis qui a fide defecerunt et sectæ acatholicæ adhæserunt. Resp. Negative ad primam partem; affirmative ad secundam.[2]

This impediment, therefore, does not affect converts to the Catholic Church, but is incurred only by fallen-away Catholics who join a non-catholic sect.

In general terms a sect is any "religious party under human unauthorized leadership."[3] A question may be raised as to what in reality constitutes a *secta acatholica* in the sense of canon 542. Is it to be restricted to an heretical or schismatical, though christian, religion, or may it be extended so as to include also the infidel and pagan religions, such as the Mohammedans, the Buddhists and the Jews? Vermeersch-Creusen[4] hold that the term must be strictly applied to include only the heretical and schismatical sects, to the exclusion of the pagan and the infidel religions. According to these authors, therefore, a catholic apostate who would join the Mohammedan religion, for example, would

[1] Biederlack-Fuehrich, *De Religiosis* p. 112.

[2] *AAS*, XI (1919), 477.

[3] Kearney, Richard Joseph, *Sponsors at Baptism according to the Code of Canon Law*, Washington, 1925, p. 83.

[4] *Epitome*, I, 390.

not incur this impediment. On the contrary, however, the spirit and aim of the impediment seems to suggest the more comprehensive interpretation, which would include in the term *secta acatholica* also the infidel and pagan religions. There seems to be little or no reason for not including them. There is just as much cause for repelling from the religious state a Catholic who joins an infidel religion, as there is for repelling the fallen-away Catholic who affiliates himself with any heretical or schismatical sect.[1]

The impediment is incurred by those fallen-away Catholics who join (*adhæserunt*) a non-catholic sect. The mere fact that one gives up the practice of his religion is not sufficient; he must, besides this, formally join one of the sects, so that *de facto*, he is a member of the sect. This requires a deliberate, wilful act; in other words, in order to incur the impediment, it is necessary that the apostate, of his own choice, had been a formal adherant of some sect opposed to the Catholic faith. His adherence must be publicly known.[2]

b) *Conjux, durante matrimonio*[3]

No married person, as long as the marriage tie exists, may validly be received as a novice in any religious community. The Code here makes a departure from the former legislation which permitted persons to become religious, if both parties consented to the separation.[4] In this case it was necessary either that both parties become religious, or that the party remaining in the world make a vow of perpetual chastity.

The Code states expressly *durante matrimonio;* hence the impediment exists until the marriage bond is either broken by death, or dissolved by a dispensation *super matrimonio non con-*

---

[1] Schaefer, *De Religiosis*, p. 263; Bakalarczyk, *De Novitiatu*, p. 57; Augustine, *Commentary*, III, 206; Maroto, *CpR*, I (1920), 162.

[2] Cappello, *Summa J. C.*, II, n. 594; Augustine, *Commentary*, III, 206; Kinane, *IER*, XV (1920), 63-67.

[3] Since the impediments of age and fear, which in the enumeration of canon 542 precede the impediment of marriage, have an express bearing on profession, they will be treated *in extenso* in a later chapter.

[4] Cf. c. 4, 12, 13, X *de conversione conjugatorum* III, 32; Schmalzgrueber, *Jus Ecclesiasticum Universum*, lib. III, tit. XXXI, n. 24; Piat, *Prælectiones Juris Regularis*, I, 62.

summato, or until the marriage is declared null and void from its very beginning. Hence according to the more common opinion of authorites[1] there is no ground for stating that the impediment ceases to exist if, according to canons 1129 §1 or 1131 §1, a perpetual separation is granted. Some canonists, however, hold the opposite opinion.[2]

c) *Qui obstringuntur vel obstricti fuerunt vinculo professionis religiosæ*

The bond of previous profession is another impediment which hinders the valid reception of candidates for the novitiate. Canon 542 states that this impediment affects all who are bound (*obstringuntur*), or who have at any time been bound (*obstricti fuerunt*), by the vows of religion.

The first part of this impediment is applicable to apostate and fugitive religious, and to all who have received the indult of exclaustration.[3] Apostates from the religious state are those professed religious who either unlawfully leave the monastery or convent with the intention of not returning, or who, though lawfully outside the monastic precincts, refuse to return.[4] Those religious are called fugitives who unlawfully leave the enclosure but with the intention of returning.[5] The indult of exclaustration permits a religious, for a just reason, to live outside his monastery or convent, either for a definite period of time, or for life, but it does not free him from his vows or from any other obligation contracted by his profession.[6]

Those persons who were at one time professed religious, labor under the same diriment impediment should they again wish to

---

[1] Blat, *Commentarium*, II, 522; Pruemmer, *Manuale J. C.*, q. 209; Mothon, *Institutions Canoniques*, II, 600; Augustine, *Commentary*, III, 209; *Jus Pontificium*, IX (1929), 94; Woywod, *Practical Commentary*, I, 214.

[2] Cappello, *Summa J. C.* II, 599; Leitner, *Handbuch des k. Kirchenrechts*, II, 395; Schaefer, in his earlier work, *Ordensrecht*, p. 152, also held this view; but in his *De Religiosis*, p. 266, he adopts the more common opinion of canonists.

[3] Fanfani, *De Jure Religiosorum*, p. 198; Pejska, *Jus Canonicum Religiosorum*, p. 80; Schaefer, *De Religiosis*, p. 267.

[4] Can. 644, §1.

[5] Can. 644, §3.

[6] Can. 638 and 639.

embrace religious life. Under this class must be enumerated all religious who have been secularized by an indult from the Holy See;[1] all who have been dispensed from their religious vows; those who either have been dismissed from their community, or who, at the expiration of their temporal profession, have left the monastic life of their own choice.[2] It matters not whether these ex-religious wish to reenter their former community, or whether they intend to enter some other order or congregation; the impediment is present in either case.[3]

The Code in canon 633 makes special provisions for professed religious who desire to transfer from their present community to another community, or to some other order or congregation. There is in this case no impediment such as is spoken of in the present canon, but, according to canon 632, this transfer may not be made without the special permission of the Holy See.

d) *Hi quibus imminet poena ob grave delictum commissum de quo accusati sunt vel accusari possunt.*

The reason why the Church debars certain criminals from the religious state, is not so much because of the crime committed, as because of the name and reputation of the religious community which is at stake. This is evident from the very nature of the impediment itself. The impediment is incurred not because of the crime committed, but because of the impending punishment due to the crime. The Church, however, in imposing this impediment, intends to hinder any frustration of the due course of justice, and at the same time to keep out of the religious state any undesirable persons who, in the words of Sixtus V, "desire to enter the religious state in order to escape the law and the severity of the judges."[4] The crime must be a grave one. Sixtus V, in his constitutions, "*Cum de omnibus*,"[5] and "*Ad Romanum spectat*,"[6] mentions such serious offenses as murder, robbery, and the

[1] Can. 640, §1, 1°, 2°.

[2] Fanfani, *De Jura Religiosorum*, p. 198; Pejska, *Jus Canonicum Religiosorum*, p. 80; Schaefer, *De Religiouss*, p. 267.

[3] Fanfani, *loc. cit.*, Woywod, *Practical Commentary*, I, 214; *HPR*, XXVII, 290; Augustine, *Commentary*, III, 210; Papi, *Religious in Church Law*, p. 178.

[4] Const. "*Cum de omnibus*," IV—*Fontes*, n. 162.

[5] *Fontes*, n. 162.

[6] *Fontes*, n. 164.

like. The Code specifies no particular crime; hence any serious offense, no matter what its nature, must be included. The crime must, moreover, be public and certain.[1] The crime may be either against the ecclesiastical, or against the civil law.[2] But in order to incur the impediment in question, the commission of the crime alone is not sufficient. It is further required that there be danger of a penalty being levied upon the offender who has either been accused or can be accused. This danger of penalty must be proximate, since the Code states *quibus imminet poena.* Hence if the criminal has already made due satisfaction for his crime, the impediment ceases to exist. This likewise holds good if a person, though guilty, has been acquitted in a court of justice.[3]

e) *Episcopus sive residentialis sive titularis, licet a Romano Pontifice sit tantum designatus*

Canonists advance various reasons for this impediment. Some state that bishops may not validly become religious without the permission of the Holy See, because the episcopacy is a state of perfection acquired, and in consequence it would be a step from a higher to a lower degree of perfection if a bishop would enter the religious state, since the latter is a state in which perfection is to be sought after.[4] Pejska does not agree with this view, and states the reason for the impediment lies in the episcopal dignity, which should not be made subject in obedience to a religious superior.[5] Pirhing[6] and Schaefer[7] contend that it is

---

[1] Schaefer, *De Religiosis*, p. 268; Papi, *Religious in Church Law*, p. 179; Fanfani, *De Jure Religiosorum*, p. 199; Cappello, *Summa J. C.*, II, n. 599.

[2] Piat, *Prælectiones Juris Regulares*, I, 72; Cappello, *Summa J. C.*, II, n. 548; De Meester, *Compendium*, II, 991; Fanfani, *De Jure Religiosorum*, p. 199;; Leitner, *Handbuch des k. Kirchenrechts*, III, 395; Vermeersch-Creusen, *Epitome*, I, 392; Pruemmer, *Manuale J. C.*, q. 204; Brandys, *Kirchliches Rechtsbuch*, p. 12; Augustine, *Commentary*, III, 210. Against these authorities, Blat, *Commentarium*, II, 523, limits the impediment to crimes committed against the civil law.

[3] Fanfani, *loc. cit.*, Cappello; *Summa J. C.*, II, n. 599; Augustine, *Commentary*, III, 210–211.

[4] Reiffenstuel, *Jus Canonicum Universum*, tom. III, lib. III, tit. XXXI, n. 76; Fanfani, *De Jure Religiosorum*, p. 199.

[5] *Jus Canonicum Religiosorum*, p. 81.

[6] *Jus Canonicum*, lib. III, tit. 31, n. 125.

[7] *De Religiosis*, p. 268.

the intimate connection which exists between the bishop and his see. Bulliart gives as his reason the existence of a tacit vow of perpetual obedience to the Pope which the bishop makes at his consecration.[1]

The impediment is extended to both residential and titular bishops; but according to Vermeersch-Creusen,[2] it does not bind bishops who have resigned, provided they have not been appointed to some titular See. In order that his impediment become effective, episcopal consecration is not necessary. Just as soon as the bishop-elect receives from the Holy See the official notification of his appointment to a residential, or to a titular bishopric, the impediment arises.[3] A special permission from the Pope is required in order that one thus designated, be able to enter the religious state.[4]

f) *Clerici qui ex instituto Sanctæ Sedis jurejurando tenentur operam suam navare in bonum suæ diocesis vel missionum, pro tempore quo obligatio jurisjurandi perdurat*

In order to alleviate the great need for priests felt in various countries, there have been established, under the auspices of the Holy See, colleges and seminaries to educate priests to fill these needs. At their entrance into these institutions, the students bind themselves by oath to serve for a given period of time, a particular diocese or mission; they promise at the same time not to enter the religious state.[5] This oath is not, however, to be confused with the one mentioned in canon 981, §1. This canon directs

---

[1] *Cursus Theologiæ*, tom. VI, Dissert. IV, art. 1.

[2] *Epitome*, I, 393.

[3] Vermeersch-Creusen, *Epitome*, I, 392; Vermeersch, *Theologia Moralis*, tom. III, lib. 1, tract II, tit. IV, cap. I, n. 116; Schaefer, *De Religiosis*, p. 268.

[4] Schmalzgrueber, *Jus Ecclesiasticum Univ.*, Tom. III, pars IV, tit. XXXI, n. 31, gives six reasons which may induce the Pope to grant a dispensation: 1) conscientia criminis; 2) debilitas corporis; 3) defectus scientiæ necessariæ; 4) malitia plebis; 5) grave scandalum; 6) irregularitas personæ non dispensabilis.

[5] The oath in part is as follows: "Insuper spondeo, et juro, dum in hoc collegio permanebo, et postquam ab eo quocumque modo, sive completis sive non completis studiis exiero, nullam Religionem, Societatem aut Congregationem Regularem sine speciali Sedis Apostolicæ licentia, vel Sacræ Congregationis de Propaganda Fide ingrediar, neque in earum aliquam professionem emittam...", Alexander VII, const. "*Cum circa,*" 20 Jul. 1660—*Fontes*, n. 237.

that, if a candidate for major orders lacks one of the ordinary titles for ordination enumerated in canon 979, §1, the *titulus servitii diocesis*, or *missionis* is to be substituted. To obtain this title, the ordinand must take an oath that he will forever serve the diocese or mission for which he is ordained.

The diriment impediment to the religious state mentioned in the final paragraph of canon 542, 1° does not arise from the oath demanded by canon 981, §1,[1] but only from the oath taken by students of the particular colleges and seminaries referred to at the beginning of this paragraph. Charles Augustine[2] incorrectly holds that this diriment impediment arises also from the oath demanded by canon 981, §1. If this were true, then everyone advanced to major orders under the title *servitii diocesis*, or *missionis*, could not validly be admitted to a religious order or congregation without a dispensation from the Holy See. This, however, is not the case. In the very next paragraph, canon 542 states that, *servatis conditionibus*, a cleric may both validly and licitly enter a religious community. The canon makes no reference to a dispensation from the Holy See. Is the term *clerici in sacris*, of canon 542, 2°, to be limited to those ordained under the *titulus beneficii, patrimonii aut pensionis* of canon 979, §1? There is no ground for such a distinction.

§2 Impedient Impediments

a) *Clerici in sacris constituti, inconsulto loci Ordinario, aut eodem contradicente ex eo quod eorum discessus in grave animarum detrimentum cedat, quod aliter vitari minime possit.*

The Church has always permitted her secular clergy to embrace the religious state if they felt themselves so called. Already in 633, the Fourth Council of Toledo declared that bishops may not hinder their clergy from entering the religious state.[3] Later on, in 952, a Synod of Augsburg says that not only should the

[1] Vermeersch-Creusen, *Epitome*, I, 393; Vermeersch, *Theologia Moralis*, tom. III, lib. I, tract. II, tit. IV, cap. 5, n. 14; Chelodi, *Jus de Personis*, n. 265. V; Schaefer, *De Religiosis*, p. 269; Bakalarczyk, *De Novitiatu*, p. 67-68; Sipos, *Enchiridion J. C.* p. 346.

[2] *Commentary*, III, 211-212; IV, 473.

[3] Cap. unic., C. XIX, q. 1.

bishop not forbid his clergy to embrace religious life, but he ought rather, by exhortation, to encourage them to persevere in their desire.[1] Pope Benedict XIV, in his letter "*Ex quo*," of January 14, 1747,[2] declared that there is nothing to hinder a secular from entering a religious community without consulting his bishop, or even from acting contrary to the latter's wishes.

With but a few restrictions, the Code has retained the earlier legislation on this subject. According to canon 542, 2°, a secular in major orders, who wishes to embrace the religious state, must first consult his Ordinary; if in the opinion of the Ordinary, the particular cleric could not leave without grave detriment to the care of souls, he may not act contrary to the Ordinary's wishes. The dictates of this legislation affect only clerics in major orders, *clericis in sacris*, which clause comprises the orders of subdeaconship, deaconship, and priesthood. It in no way binds clerics in minor orders, who, therefore, may be both validly and licitly received into any religious community without their first consulting the Ordinary.[3] Schaefer, however, remarks that common politeness demands that such minorists at least inform the Ordinary of their intention.

Canonists are not unanimous in their interpretation of the clause *inconsulto loci ordinario*. Augustine[4] interprets it to mean that the majorist must obtain the *consent* of his Ordinary before he may licitly enter the religious state. Cappello[5] and Arendt[6] go to the other extreme by saying that it is necessary only that the cleric *inform* his Ordinary of his intention. De Meester,[7] Pejska,[8] Cocchi,[9] and Vermeersch-Creusen[10] give a more conservative interpretation, by declaring that the cleric is bound to

---

[1] C. 7.—*Mansi*, XVIII, 438.

[2] *Fontes*, n. 374; cf. also Bouix, *De Jure Regularium*, pars IV, sec. 1, cap. 1, n. 2.

[3] Pejska, *Jus Canonicum Religiosorum*, p. 81; Schaefer, *De Religiosis*, p. 270; Vermeersch, *Theol. Moralis*, tom. III, lib. 1, tract. IV.

[4] *Commentary*, III, 212.

[5] *Summa J. C.*, II, n. 601.

[6] "De Canone 542 et 981, Deque libero clericorum ingressu in religionem" —*Jus Pontificium*, IV (1924), 185.

[7] *J. C., Compendium*, II, n. 992.

[8] *Jus Canonicum Religiosorum*, p. 81.

[9] *Commentarium*, lib. II, pars II, n. 64.

[10] *Epitome*, I, 394.

ask the advice of his Ordinary, but that he need not abide by it, should he counsel against embracing the religious state. The first rule of interpretation states that the canons are to be interpreted according to the proper signification of the terms used by the legislator.[1] The term *inconsulto Ordinario*, in its proper signification, can mean nothing else than "without consulting the Ordinary," or, in other words, without asking his advice. There is no valid reason for restricting it to mean "without the *consent* of the Ordinary," as Augustine does; nor may it be extended to mean "without first *informing* the Ordinary," as Cappello and Arendt apply the term. Hence the more conservative interpretation seems to be the correct one.

The Code admits only one instance when the Ordinary may forbid entrance into the religious state, namely, if the vacancy thus created would bring serious detriment to souls. This may easily be the case in dioceses where priests are few; but especially will this occur when the proper care of souls demands a priest who is able to speak the native tongue of the people. In all such cases, the Ordinary is to judge whether or not a particular cleric's entering a religious community would cause such a detriment to the care of souls; the cleric, however, may always appeal to the Holy See against the Ordinary's decision.[2] The impediment is, however, an impedient one, so that even if in this latter case, a cleric in major orders is admitted contrary to the demands of the Bishop, his admission is valid, but illicit. Should the bishop demand that the cleric return to the diocese, the matter should be referred to the Holy See.[3]

b) *Aere alieno gravati, qui solvendo pares non sint.*

Persons who are burdened with debts which they cannot pay, may not licitly be received into the religious state. Before the Code, a grave debt (*contractum ingentem vim æris alieni*)[4] was required to incur this impediment. The Code, however, makes

---

[1] Canon 18.

[2] Pejska, *Jus Canonicum Religiosorum*, p. 81; Veermersch-Creusen, *Epitome*, I, 394; Sipos, *Enchiridion J. C.*, p. 346; Schaefer, *De Religiosis*, p. 240.

[3] Vermeersch, *Theologia Moralis*, tom. III, lib. I, tract. II, tit. IV, cap. 1, n. 115; Schaefer, *De Religiosis*, p. 271.

[4] Sixtus V, const. "*Cum de omnibus*" 26 Nov. 1584, IV,—*Fontes*, n. 162.

no such limitation; it includes any debt that could constitute a *materia gravis* in violation of justice. The debt, however, must be certain, and it must be one which arises from a valid contract, or one which is incurred through some delinquency on the part of the debtor.[1]

If the debtor has the means of paying the debt, he should do so before he is received. If it is very likely that within a reasonable time the debtor will be able to acquire sufficient means to meet his creditors, he must postpone his entrance into religious life, unless this delay would be the cause of grave spiritual detriment to the individual, or if it would result in the loss of his vocation.[2] Authorities consider that a space of two or three years is a reasonable period of time within which to liquidate a debt.[3] But should the debtor be absolutely unable to meet his creditors, and have no prospects of being able to do so, it will be necessary to petition the Holy See for a dispensation in order to admit such a person.[4] This, however, will not be necessary if the creditors consent to remit the debt.[5]

c) *Reddendæ rationi obnoxii aut aliis sæcularibus negotiis implicati, ex quibus lites et molestias religio timere possit*

Another class or persons whose licit reception into religious life is hindered by an impediment, are those engaged in the administration of temporal and secular affairs, of which they are obliged to render an account. Traces of this impediment are to be found as early as the sixth century, in the letters of Gregory the Great.[6] It is again met with in the constitutions "*Cum de omnibus*"[7] of Sixtus V, and "*Cum ad regularem*"[8] of Clement VIII.

---

[1] Fanfani, *De Jure Religiosorum*, p. 201; Schaefer, *De Religiosis*, p. 271; Bakalarczyk, *De Novitiatu*, p. 70; Piat, *Prælectiones Juris Regularis*, I, 66–67.

[2] Fanfani, *De Jure Religiosorum*, p. 201; Vermeersch-Creusen, *Epitome*, I, 249; Schmalzgrueber, *Jus Ecclesiasticum Universum*, tom. III, pars IV, tit. XXXI, n. 37.

[3] Schmalzgrueber, *Jus Ecclesiasticum Universum*, tom. III, pars IV, tit. XXXI, n. 37; Pirhing, *Jus Canonicum*, lib. VI, tit. 31, n. 130.

[4] Bakalzrczyk, *De Novitiatu*, p. 71.

[5] "Consentienti non fit injuria."—Reg. 27, R. J. in VI.

[6] Cap. unic., D. LIII.

[7] I—*Fontes*, n. 162.

[8] III—*Fontes*, n. 189.

The administration of which there is question here may be either in public or in private matters. Hence all public officials, those who have charge of the pecuniary administration of public affairs, *i.e.*, secretaries and treasurers of business concerns, come under this impediment. With these must be classed also the administrators of private affairs such as tutors, guardians, or executors of wills.[1]

In order that this impediment be incurred, it is necessary that from these administrations there be dangers of future lawsuits or other difficulties which might involve the religious community in legal strifes (*ex quibus lites et molestias religio timere possit*). The impediment ceases just as soon as all matters pertaining to such business affairs have been satisfactorily settled.

d) *Filii qui parentibus, id est patri vel matri, avo vel aviæ, in gravi necessitate constitutis, opitulari debent, et parentes quorum opera sit ad liberos alendos vel educandos necessaria*

The natural law itself demands that children aid their parents, should they fall into grave necessity. The Code, in establishing an impediment hindering the licit reception into religious life of children whose parents or grandparents are situated in grave necessity and want, only confirms the natural law.

When may it be said that this grave necessity is present? No definite rule or guide can possibly be established according to which the degree of necessity could be reckoned. Authors, however, give various norms by means of which it would be possible to arrive at a conclusion in a given case. Cocchi considers the necessity to be grave if the parents or grandparents, in order to permit their offspring to enter religion, would be obliged to place themselves at the mercy of some charitable institution.[2] According to Vermersch-Creusen, the degree of necessity required for the existence of this impediment would be present if the entrance of their child into a religious community would oblige the

---

[1] Reiffenstuel, *Jus Canonicum Universum*, tom. III, lib. III, tit. XXXI, n. 72; Schmalzgrueber, *Jus Ecclesiasticum Universum*, tom. III, pars IV, tit. XXXI, n. 25; Piat, *Prælectiones Juris Regularis*, I, 68–71; Augustine, *Commentary*, III, 213.

[2] *Commentarium*, lib. II, pars II, n. 64.

parents to undergo hardships or embarrassment which would be unbecoming to their state or condition in life.[1] All circumstances must be considered not absolutely, but relatively to the status of each individual case. If grave necessity will cause this impediment to arise, then *a fortiori* extreme necessity will do the same. The Code is, however, silent concerning the *necessitas communis;* in consequence this degree of necessity will not be sufficient to cause this impediment to arise.

Children, as long as they will be able to alleviate the grave necessity of parents by remaining in the world, may not be licitly granted admittance into a religious institute. But if, even by remaining in the world, there be no hope of bettering the condition of parents, or of relieving their necessity, the impediment ceases.[2] This impediment likewise ceases if, by their entering the religious state, such children would be enabled in some way to provide for the needs of their parents.[3]

A novice whose parents, during the term of his probation, are reduced to grave necessity, may not be advanced to profession; he must immediately return to the world. If this necessity arises only after the candidate has already made his profession, the question takes on a different aspect. Must he leave the religious institute to provide for his parents? Authors here generally distingusih between grave and extreme necessity. The probable opinion holds that if the necessity of the parents is only grave, the professed religious is not obliged to return to the world. If, however, the necessity of the parents is extreme, and there is no other way of alleviation, the professed religious must return to the world to assist his parents.[4] But if the religious institute is

---

[1] *Epitome*, I, 395–396.

[2] Reiffenstuel, *Jus Canonicum Universum*, tom. III, lib. III, tit. XXXI, n. 77; Piat, *Prælectiones Juris Regularis*, I, 52; Leitner, *Handbuch*, III, 396; Pejska, *Jus Canonicum Religiosorum*, p. 82.

[3] Fanfani, *De Jure Religiosorum*, p. 202; Biederlack-Fuehrich, *De Religiosis*, p. 122; Piat, *op. cit.*, I, 53; Leitner, *op. cit.*, III, 392.

[4] Piat, *op. cit.*, I, 54; Pirhing, *Jus Canonicum*, lib. III, tit. XXXI, n. 128; Fanfani, *De Jure Religiosorum*, p. 202; Schaefer, *De Religiosis*, p.. 272; Vermeersch, *Theologia Moralis*, tom.. III, lib. I, tract. II, tit. IV, cap. 1, n. 115; Pruemmer, *Manuale J. C.*, q. 205; Vermeersch-Creusen, *Epitome*, I, 396; Biederlack-Fuehrich, *De Religiosis*, p. 123; Noldin, *De Præceptis*, n. 286.

both able and willing to assist the parents and thus relieve their wants, the religious need not give up his chosen life.[1]

The second part of this impediment has reference to parents who wish to consecrate themselves to God in the religious state. Parents have a strict obligation to rear their children. It is their bounden duty to provide for the spiritual, intellectual, and bodily needs of their offspring.[2] Until this duty has been accomplished to its fullest extent, no parent may be received into a religious community.

e) *Ad sacerdotium in Religione destinati, a quo tamen removeantur irregularitate aliove canonico impedimento.*

This impediment to religious life is applicable only to those candidates who enter a religious community with the intention of being advanced to sacred orders. The young man who wishes to be ordained must be free from all irregularities and simple impediments. Irregularities may be either *ex defectu*, or *ex delicto*. Canon 984, of the Code, lists the following as irregular *ex defecto:* 1) illegitimates; 2) those afflicted with some bodily defect or deformity on account of which they cannot safely or with decorum, perform the sacred functions of the priesthood; 3) epileptics, the insane and those possessed by the devil; 4) those who have contracted two or more valid marriages; 5) persons who have by law incurred the loss of their good name; 6) judges who have pronounced sentence of death; 7) executioners, and those who voluntarily assumed the office of immediate assistants at executions.

According to canon 985, the following are irregular *ex delicto:* 1) apostates, heretics, and schismatics; 2) persons who, except in the case of extreme necessity, permitted themselves to be baptized by a non-catholic; 3) those who attempted marriage, or went through the civil formalities of marriage, when they were already living in valid marriage, after they had received major orders, or after having made simple or solemn religious profession; those are likewise irregular who attempt marriage with a married

[1] Pruemmer, *Manuale J. C.*, q. 205; Fanfani, *De Jure Religiosorum*, p. 202; Schaefer, *De Religiosis*, p. 273.

[2] Cf. Can. 1113.

woman, or with a religious of either simple or solemn vows; 4) those guilty of voluntary homicide; those guilty of effectively procuring abortion, or who co-operated in the crime; 5) persons who have mutilated themselves, or who have attempted suicide; 6) clerics practicing medicine or surgery, if thereby the death of a person has occurred; 7) those who have usurped the exercise of an act reserved to one in major orders; likewise clerics in major orders who have exercised their orders when they had been forbidden to do so by canonical penalty.

The following, according to canon 987, are hindered by impediments to holy orders: 1) the sons of non-catholics, as long as the parents remain in their error; 2) married men; 3) officials and adminstrators, as long as they hold an office forbidden to the clergy; 4) slaves, before they have been granted their liberty; 5) persons bound to military service; 6) converts until, according to the judgment of the Ordinary, they have given sufficient proof of their faith; 7) persons who, because of some crime, labor under ill repute, until they have, in the judgment of the bishop, regained their good name.

Of these irregularities and impediments, some are permanent, while others are only temporary in character. Only such irregularities will hinder entrance into the religious state which are permanent. Irregularities which will cease in due time, such as age, or those which may be removed by profession, such as illegitimacy—which is removed when the religious makes solemn profession[1]—are not included in this impediment to the religious state.[2]

Must a dispensation from the otherwise permanent irregularity be obtained before the candidate may be received? Authors are not unanimous in their response to this question. According to Fanfani[3], if the irregularity is one from which a dispensation is easily obtainable, there is no necessity of seeking the dispensation before admitting the candidate. Other authorities

---

[1] Can. 984, 1°.

[2] Fanfani, *De Jure Religiosorum*, p. 202; Vermeersch-Creusen, *Epitome*, I, 397; Vermeersch, *Theol. Moralis*, tom. III, lib. 1, tract. III, tit. IV, cap. 1, n. 115; Schaefer, *De Religiosis*, p. 273; Bakalarczyk, *De Novitiatu*, p. 75; Voltas, *CpR*, II (1921), 369.

[3] *De Jure Religiosorum*, p. 203.

hold that in all instances must the dispensation be obtained before the candidate may licitly be received.[1] Of the two opinions, the latter is the more logical. The canon in question states that those who labor under such an irregularity may not be licitly received into any religious community as candidates for the priesthood. It is only by a dispensation that such an irregularity is removed. Therefore, since the reception of such candidates will be illicit as long as they are bound by the irregularity, the only way to render their reception licit is to obtain the necessary dispensation. Voltas' remark is to the point:

> **Hinc licet nemini causam S. Sedi reservatam judicio suo prævertere et sua agendi ratione quasi præoccupare. Perperam igitur Superiores agerent si, judicio supremæ auctoritatis præeuntes, ad novitiatum in statu clericali admitterent illum qui irregularitate aliove canonico impedimento irretetur, quamvis ejus dispensatio, ut speratur, sit obtentu facilis.**[2]

But in case the candidate has nevertheless been admitted without first obtaining the dispensation, it will be sufficient to seek the necessary dispensation before the conferring of the clerical tonsure.

f) *Orientales in latinis religionibus sine venia scripto data Sacræ Congregationis pro Ecclesia Orientali.*

This impediment, which states that Orientals may not enter a religious institute of the Latin rite without the written permission of the Holy See, is but an amplification of canon 98, §3, which forbids a change of rite without first having recourse to the Holy See. This impediment does not, however, hinder the reception of such Orientals who, without changing their rite, wish to enter a novitiate in the Latin rite, for the purpose of preparing themselves to found houses or provinces for their own rite.[3]

---

[1] Vermeersch-Creusen, *Epitome*, I, 396–397; Vermeersch, *Theologia Moralis*, tom. III, lib. I, tract. III, cap. 1, n. 115; Pruemmer, *Manuale J. C.*, q. 205; Bakalarczyk, *De Noviatu*, p. 75; Voltas, *CpR*, II (1921), 368.

[2] *CpR*, II (1921), 368.

[3] Com. Interp., 10 Nov. 1925—*AAS*, XVII (1925), 582.

CHAPTER V

GENERAL REQUIREMENTS FOR THE VALIDITY OF PROFESSION

The requirements for the validity of every religious profession are enumerated in canon 572 §1, of the Code, in the following words:

Ad validitatem cujusvis religiosæ professionis requiritur ut:

1. **Qui eam emissurus est, legitimam ætatem habeat ad normam can. 573;**
2. **Eum ad professionem admittat legitimus Superior secundum constitutiones;**
3. **Novitiatus validus ad normam can. 555 præcesserit;**
4. **Professio sine vi aut metu gravi aut dolo emittatur;**
5. **Sit expressa;**
6. **A legitimo Superiore secundum constitutiones per se vel per alium recipiatur.**

§1 Age

Before setting down the requirements of present legislation dealing with the age required of candidates for religious profession, it will be of interest to cast a passing glance at former customs and ecclesiastical prescriptions on this point. In the early periods of the Church—before the fourth century—no age requirement was in existence. Children of tenderest years were permitted to be consecrated to God. St. Ambrose[1] remarks that the Church considered not so much the number of years of natural life, but rather the *ætatem fidei et pudoris*. St. Jerome, in his twenty-fourth epistle,[2] relates that a certain maiden named

[1] *De Virg.*, n. 39—*MPL*, XVI, 276.
[2] *MPL*, XXII, 427.

Asella consecrated her life to God when she was scarcely ten years old. Irene, the sister of Pope St. Damasus, although she died at the age of twenty years, had already spent many years as a consecrated spouse of Christ.[1] St. Benedict devotes an entire chapter to the reception of children. The parents of such children, he directs, must make the necessary promises in their stead. The written formula, similar to the one demanded for the profession of novices, together with the obligations and the hand of the child were then to be enfolded in the altar-cloth as a sign of the child's complete dedication to God.[2]

Early ecclesiastical legislation was not uniform in establishing the age required for entering religious life. The synod of Saragossa (380),[3] and that of Agde (506),[4] prohibited the veiling of any virgin before she had attained the age of forty years. The Third Council of Carthage (397) forbade the consecration of virgins before the age of twenty-five.[5]

Because of the austerity of monastic life, Pope St. Gregory the Great, in a letter written to Athenus, demanded that a youth must have completed his eighteenth year before he could be received as a monk.[6] The Council of Trullo (692), however, considered a profession valid if it was made after the age of ten years.[7] Egbert, Archbishop of York, in 748 declared that no one was permitted to become a monk unless he was fifteen years old.[8] The Synods of Oxford, in 1222,[9] and of Rheims, in 1231,[10] declared that under no consideration could profession be made before the candidate had attained the age of eighteen years. Pope Innocent IV (1243–1254), on the other hand, recognized the validity of profession made at the age of fifteen years. He stated that if a youth entered a monastic community before the age of fourteen, he would be free to leave unless he made profession during his fifteenth year.[11]

---

1 *MPL*, XIII, 405.

2 *Regula S. Benedicti*, c. 59.

3 C. 4.—*Mansi*, III, 880.

4 C. 19,—*Mansi*, VIII, 328.

5 C. 5, D. 77.

6 *Mansi*, IX, 1068.

7 C. 40,—*Hefele*, III, 336.

8 *Mansi*, XII, 438.

9 C. 43,—*Mansi*, XXII, 1164.

10 *Hefele*, V, 1010.

11 C. 1, *de regularibus et transeuntibus ad religionem*, III, 14, in VI°.

The Council of Trent brought a much needed regulation in this matter. This Council was the first to enact a universal law demanding a definite minimum age for the validity of religious profession. It declared:

In quacumque religione tam virorum quam mulierum, professio non fiat ante decimum sextum annum expletum...Professio autem antea facta sit nulla, nullamque inducat obligationem ad alicujus regulæ vel religionis vel ordinis observationem, aut ad alios quoscumque effectus.[1]

The age of sixteen, established by this Council, for valid profession, continued to be the minimum age for all clerical novices. A new regulation was later on established for lay brothers. Clement VIII, in his constitution "*Cum ad Regularem*," of March 19, 1603,[2] demanded that they be at least twenty-one years old before they could be admitted to make their profession. A similar requirement was made by the Sacred Congregation of Religious in the decree "*Sacrosancta*," of January 1, 1911.[3]

The present age requirement for profession is stated in canon 573 of the Code. It reads:

Quilibet professionem religiosam emissurus oportet ut decimum sextum ætatis annum expleverit, si de temporaria professione agatur; vicesimum primum, si de perpetua sive sollemni sive simplici.

The first part of this canon repeats the law of the Council of Trent, but the second part, establishing a definite minimum age for perpetual profession, is an entirely new piece of legislation. At the time of the Council of Trent, solemn profession alone was in existence. In consequence therefore, the age of sixteen years, as established by this Council, was the age for making solemn profession. Later on, however, because of the encyclical of Pius IX, "*Neminem Latet*," issued on March 19, 1857, it became necessary that solemn profession be preceded by simple profession, which was to extend over a period of three years. This new legislation necessitated a change in the age requirement. Sixteen years now became the age for making simple profession, while

---

[1] Sessio XXV, *de reg. et mon.*, cap. 15.

[2] *Fontes*, n. 189.

[3] *AAS*, III (1911), 29.

solemn profession could be made at the age of nineteen years.[1] For lay-brothers, however, the age for making solemn profession was advanced to twenty-four years, because of the prescriptions of the constitution of Clement VII, "*Cum ad Regularem*," referred to above.

The Code, in establishing sixteen years as the age for making temporary profession, and twenty-one years for solemn profession, uniformly regulates the minimum age at which any religious may validly make profession. In the age requirement there is no longer the distinction between the profession of clerical and lay religious; canon 573 is the norm for all religious, be they male or female, clerical or lay. This is evident from the introductory clause of canon 572: *ad validitatem quælibet religiosæ professionis*, and from the opening words of canon 573: *quilibet professionem religiosam emissurus*. From this it follows that former legislation of the constitution "*Cum ad Regularem*," and of the decree "*Sacrosancta*" are no longer in force, because they are contrary to the prescriptions of the Code and, therefore, in accordance with canon 6, 1°,[2] are abrogated.[3] When stating, however, that canon 573 is the norm for all religious, it must be borne in mind that this canon regulates only the *minimum* age; it does not preclude the establishing of a higher age requirement by the constitution of any individual religious institute. Therefore, if a particular religious institute, in its constitution, prescribes that its candidates must be 18, 20, or more years of age before being admitted to profession, those prescriptions of the particular constitution must be observed under pain of nullifying the profession.[4] If, according to such constitutions, the age required for the first profession is advanced so that the required three years of temporary profession are impossible before the age of twenty-

---

[1] Bachofen, *Compendium Juris Regularium*, p. 84; Piat, *Prælectiones Juris Regularium*, I, 139.

[2] "Leges quælibet, sive universales sive particulares, præscriptis hujus Codicis oppositæ, abrogantur, nisi de particularibus legibus aliud expresse caveatur."—Can. 6, 1°.

[3] S. C. de Rel. Oct. 6, 1919—*AAS*, XI (1919), 420; Schaefer, *De Religiosis*, p. 331; Pruemmer, *Manuale, J.C.* q. 213; Leitner, *Handbuch*, III, 414; Woywod, *Practical Commentary*, I, 236.

[4] Schaefer, *De Religiosis*, p. 331; Vermeersch-Creusen, *Epitome*, I, 425; Augustine, *Commentary* III, 255; Cance, *Le Code*, II, 90.

one is completed, then, *ipso facto*, the age necessary for validly making perpetual profession in that institute will likewise be advanced. But if, on the other hand, the constitutions change only the age for perpetual profession, it would not necessarily follow that the age for making the first profession would also be changed. Consequently, unless the constitutions make other provisions, the first profession may validly be made at the completion of the sixteenth year.[1]

The age, as required by the present legislation, must be completed before the profession may validly be made. In computing the age of the candidate, the general norms for the computation of time as set down in canon 34 §3, 3°,[2] must be followed. This canon teaches that in computing a period of time when the terminus *a quo* does not coincide with the beginning of the day, which, according to canon 32, is midnight,[3] the first day is not to be counted; the period of time in question will then be completed at the close (*i.e.*, midnight) of the anniversary day. To illustrate: if the candidate for profession was born on January 1, 1910, his sixteenth year, according to the norms of computation, will be complete at the close of his sixteenth birthday, or, in other words, at midnight, between January 1 and 2, 1926, so that his profession may not take place until the morning of January 2, 1926.

§2 Admission by Proper Authority

A second qualification for the validity of profession is, that the candidate must be admitted to profession by the legitimate superiors. Admission to profession is antecedent to the profession itself, and signifies the act whereby the properly authorized superior gives assent to the profession, or in other words, gives permission to the candidate to make profession. The convenience, or rather, the necessity of this manifestation of consent on the part of the superior, is evident from the nature of profession. Profession is a contract between two parties, the candidate and the religious institute. Just as for any other contract, so also

---

[1] Creusen, *Periodica*, XII (1923), 57.

[2] "Si terminus *a quo* non coincidat cum initio diei...primus dies ne computetur et tempus finiatur expleto ultimo die ejusdem numeri."—C. 34 §3, 3°.

[3] "Dies constat 24 horis continuo supputandis a media nocte..."—Can. 32.

for religious profession is the consent of both parties necessary for its validity. The religious community which admits the candidate to profession takes upon itself the obligation of providing for every professed member, an obligation which cannot be imposed unless the community consents.

Not any and every person may enter into a contract, but those only to whom this right is granted by law. The right to admit novices to profession is vested in the major superiors conjointly with either their council or chapter, according to the prescriptions of the institute's constitutions.[1]

The major superiors, as understood in the prescriptions of canon 543, are the Abbot Primate, the Abbot Superior or President of a congregation, the Abbot regiminis of autonomous monasteries, the Superior-general, the Provincial Superiors or their Vicars, and any others who may be invested with like jurisdiction as the Provincials.[2] To this list must be added the Conventual Prior, who is the superior of an autonomous monastery which lacks the abbatial dignity, and those Superiors of such orders as the Camaldulese or Carthusians, who do not permit the use of the name "abbot."[3] Canon 490 teaches that, except where the context would rule otherwise, the canons governing religious in general apply equally to religious women. This being the case, religious Superioresses are also to be classed among the major superiors,[4] and therefore in accordance with the prescrip-

---

[1] "Jus admittendi ad novitiatum et subsequentem professionem religiosam tam temporariam quam perpetuam pertinet ad Superiores majores cum suffragio consilii seu capituli secundum peculiares cujusque religionis constitutiones."—Can. 543.

[2] "In canonibus quæ sequuntur, veniunt nomine superiorum majorum: Abbas primas, abbas superior congregationis monasticæ, abbas monasterii sui juris, licet ad monasticam congregationem pertinentis, supremus religionis moderator, superior provincialis, eorumque vicarii aliique ad instar provincialium potestatem habentes."—Can. 488, 8°.

[3] "Duplex saltem responsum Commissionis novimus ex quo constat et *Priores conventuales in congregationibus monasticis et Superiores domorum* sui juris in *Religionibus monasticis centralizatis*, inter Superiores majores recenseri posse."—Larraona, *CpR*, IV (1923), 41. In a footnote the author states that he has reference to private unpublished responses of the Commission.

[4] Vermeersch-Creusen, *Epitome*, I, 343; Fanfani, *De Jure Religiosorum*, p. 57; Schaefer, *De Religiosis*, p. 124; Larraona, *CpR*, IV (1923), 42 sqq; *Jus Pontificium*, VII (1927), 11.

tions of canon 543, likewise have the right to admit novices to profession.[1] To determine in a particular case which superior *de facto* is invested with this right, it will be necessary to have recourse to the constitutions of each particular order or congregation; this is apparent from the concluding words of the canon in question: *secundum peculiares cujusque religionis constitutiones.*

In connection with this point, a very practical question presents itself for consideration: are the local Ordinaries to be included among those who have the right to admit candidates to profession? This question has its application especially in reference to orders and congregations of women. The power of the ordinary over the religious institutes of his diocese does not extend itself to the internal government of these institutes. As the Ordinary of the diocese, he has power *over* these religious in accordance with the various canons of the Code, but the internal government remains with the communities themselves.[2] Now the admission of candidates to the novitiate and to their subsequent profession is preeminently a part of the internal government, and consequently the right to admit candidates to both the novitiate and to profession belongs to those in whom is vested the internal government, or in accordance with canon 543, to the major superiors, with the advice of their chapter or council. The major superiors, as seen above, are those enumerated in canon 488, 8°. Since in the enumeration of this canon there is no mention made of local Ordinaries, it must be concluded that they have, by common law, no right in the admission of candidates to profession, with the exception of the right to examine into the free status of candidates for institutes of women; this latter right is expressly granted in canon 552 §2. And since, moreover, in designating the major superiors of religious institutes as the legitimate superiors for admitting candidates, canon 543 makes no distinction between the various kinds of institutes, the above conclusion is applicable to institutes of both pontifical and diocesan right. The reason for this is quite evident. All

[1] Schmalzgrueber, *Jus Ecclesiasticum Universum*, tom. III, pars. IV, tit. XXXI, n. 186; Fanfani, *De Jure Religiosorum*, p. 57.

[2] "...non recte ab aliquibus affirmari Ordinarium, vi suæ plenæ potestatis, verum Superiorem supremum *internum*...constituti. Postestas Ordinarii est perfecta in suo genere, non tamen *formaliter interna* sed externa..."—Larraona, *CpR*, V (1924), 148.

societies or institutes whose members make public vows, whether temporal or perpetual, are religious institutes in the strict interpretation of the term.[1] Therefore all such institutes, whether they be of pontifical or of diocesan right, are equally governed by the canons of the Code referring to religious, unless these canons expressly make other provisions. Since in canon 543, no such particular provision is made, it is evident that its prescriptions apply equally to all religious institutes.[2]

Just as in all matters of great import, so also in the admission of candidates to profession, the superior must act conjointly with either the chapter or council, according to the dictates of the individual constitutions. It is the entire community or institute which becomes obligated, and therefore the community, through its representatives, has a right to voice its opinion as to whether or not it desires to bind itself to the obligations contracted in virtue of each new profession. This right is exercised by means of what canon 543 styles the *suffragium concilii seu capituli*. This vote may be either deliberative or consultative. It is deliberative when the *consent* of the council or chapter is precsribed in order that the superior may act; it is consultative when only the *advice* is necessary. In the former case, the superior is bound to act in accordance with the vote; to act otherwise would be to act invalidly. When, however, only the consultative vote is prescribed, the superior need not abide by the vote returned, but may, if prudence dictates otherwise, act contrary to it.[3]

For admitting novices to their first profession, a deliberative vote is required; but when there is question of admission to perpetual profession, whether simple or solemn, only a consultative vote is prescribed,[4] with this exception, that when a candidate

---

[1] Can. 488, 1°.

[2] Cf. Schaefer, *De Religiosis*, p. 276; Vermeersch-Creusen, *Epitome*, I, 399; Fanfani, *De Juro Religiosorum*, p. 219; Bakalarczyk, *De Novitiatu*, p. 79; Woywod, *Practical Commentary*, I, 216; Cappello, *Summa J. C.*, II, n. 611.

[3] "Si consensus exigatur, superior contra earundem votum invalide agit; si consilium tantum...satis est ad valide agendum ut superior illas personas audit; quamvis nulla obligatione teneatur ad eorum votum etsi concors, accedendi..."—Can. 105, 1°.

[4] Can. 575, §2.

for perpetual profession is received by transfer from another order or congregation, according to the prescriptions of canon 634, the vote is deliberative.[1]

According to the prescriptions therefore, of canon 575 §2, the superior must act in accordance with the decision of the chapter, as expressed by their vote, when there is question of admission to the first profession, even though personally he holds views contrary to the will of the chapter. Consequently to admit to his first profession, one whom the chapter refused to admit, would be to act invalidly; the profession would be null and void.[2] At the same time, the superior who would act in this manner, would subject himself to severe punishment, not excluding the deprivation of office, according to the gravity of his fault.[3] But when there is question of admitting to perpetual profession, the superior, after receiving the advice may, if he sees fit, either receive or reject a candidate without following the vote returned.

It may seem odd, at first sight, that the vote for temporary profession should be deliberate, while for perpetual profession it is only consultative. Canonists advance various reasons in explanation of this point. Vermeersch-Creusen state that the reason for making perpetual profession a matter of consultative vote only is to safeguard the right which the worthy temporarily-professed religious has to perpetual profession.[4] Toso[5] advances as a plausible reason the fact that for temporary profession there is question of receiving a candidate *into* the community, whereas in the case of perpetual profession there is question only of confirming the status of the religious *in* the community. Woywood thinks that, for all practical purposes, it should matter little whether the vote for perpetual profession is deliberative or consultative. The reasons he advances are well worth quoting:

Every major superior... realizes the importance of admitting to perpetual membership those only who have proved themselves worthy... Wherefore if a candidate for perpetual profession receives a bare plurality of votes...the major superior...should take warning and not burden

---

[1] Comm. Interp., 14 Jul. 1922,—*AAS*, X, (1922) 526.
[2] *IER*, XXI (1923), 305.
[3] Can. 2411.
[4] *Epitome*, I, 423.
[5] *Commentaria Minora*, p. 149.

the community with an unfit character. In such a case the present law is far better than if the council could decide the admission by an absolute plurality of votes...In the ordinary, common-sense acceptance of a vote on the character and vocation of a candidate for perpetual membership, the bare plurality of votes in his favor leave doubtful the advisability of accepting him, and if this be doubtful he should not be accepted.[1]

After the chapter has decided in favor of the novice's admission to profession, it may happen that the profession must, for one reason or another, be delayed. The question arises whether or not the novice must be submitted to a second canvass at the end of the delay, before he may pronounce his temporary vows. If the cause of the postponement has no bearing on the fitness of the novice, and the delay is of short duration, there seems to be no necessity of a second canvass. But if the postponement took place because some doubt arose as to the fitness of the novice, it is quite evident that the chapter must again decide by vote whether or not he is to be admitted.[2] The case will be somewhat different when there is question of a postponement of perpetual profession after the chapter has given its consultative vote in favor of advancing the temporarily professed religious to perpetual vows. In this case a second canvass is not required.[3]

§3 Valid Novitiate

The Council of Trent very solemnly declared that no religious profession could be valid or obligatory in any respect, unless it had been preceded by an entire year of probation.[4] The Code likewise prescribes a valid novitiate as an essential prerequisite for profession.[5]

Three conditions must be fulfilled that a novitiate may be valid: 1. The candidate must have completed the fifteenth year of his age, and must be free from invalidating impediments.

---

[1] *HPR*, XXX (1930), 985–986.

[2] Goyeneche, *CpR*, III (1922), 219, sq.; Pejska, *Jus Canonicum Religiosorum*, pp. 105, sq.

[3] S. C. Ep., et Reg. 18 Aug. 1905.—*Fontes*, n. 2051.

[4] Sess. XXV, *de reg. et monial.*, cap. 15.

[5] Can. 572 §1, 3°.

2. The novitiate must extend over an entire, continuous year.
3. It must be made in the house set aside for the novitiate.[1]

It is beyond the scope of this dissertation to enter into a detailed discussion of these points; but a few words in explanation of the second point may not be amiss. In the first place, the novitiate must extend over the space of an entire year. In computing the year, the prescriptions of canon 34, §3, 3°, must be followed.[2] According to the directions given in this canon, the year of novitiate is not completed until the close of the anniversary day of the investiture, so that a novice who was invested on January 1, may not validly make his profession until January 2 of the following year. Besides being an entire year, the year of novitiate must also be continuous, that is, without interruption. This requirement must, however, be interpreted in the light of canon 556, which states that if a novice, for any reason whatsoever, is absent from the novitiate house for a space of more than thirty days, whether continuous or at differnet intervals, the novitiate is broken and, consequently, must be recommenced. But if a space of more than fifteen days, but not exceeding thirty days is thus spent outside the precincts of the novitiate, that exact number of days must be supplied before the novice may validly be admitted to profession. Finally, if the absence did not exceed fifteen days, the superior may prescribe that these days be supplied, but this is not necessary for the validity of the novitiate.[3]

Some religious institutes prescribe more than one year of probation. This extra time is not, however, required for the validity of the novitiate, unless this is expressly stated in the constitutions.[4] The Sacred Congregation has issued an instruction concerning this second year of probation in which it is stated that when this second year is spent outside of the novitiate house, the novices must return to the same two months in advance of the day set for their profession. These two months are to be devoted exclusively to preparation for the profession.[5]

---

[1] Can. 555 §1.
[2] Comm. Interp., 12 Nov. 1922. ad. 1.—*AAS*, XIV (1922), 661.
[3] Can. 556 §2.
[4] Can. 555 §2.
[5] S. C. de Rel., 3 Nov. 1921.—*AAS*, XIII (1921), 539.

§4 Freedom of Action

To consecrate oneself to the Divine Master through religious profession, is a step of great importance. It requires the full and perfect consent of the candidate. Hence, also the Code considers violence, fear, and deceit, sufficient to vitiate the consent to such an extent that profession, made under the influence of any of them, is null and void.

1. Violence is defined as "an onset of force too great to be resisted,[1] or as Noldin says,[2] it is the force resorted to in order to compel another to act. A person who acts under violence is not the master of his own act; he acts rather as the mere tool of a second person.

Any act performed by a person under the influence of irresistible violence from without, is considered as though it had not been performed.[3] Consequently, should a person go through the entire act of making religious profession, pronounce the vows of religion, sign the documents, acting not of his own volition, but because of violence exerted upon him by some extrinsic cause, that profession would be null and void, it would produce absolutely no obligations either in the external forum, or in the forum of conscience.

2. Fear is a "perturbation of the mind arising from present or future danger."[4] Fear may be *grave*, or *slight*, according as the impending danger causing the fear is either serious or slight. To constitute grave fear, two conditions must be verified: the evil causing the fear must be great, and it must be difficult to escape. Fear may be *just* or *unjust*. It is just, when the author of the fear has a right to inflict the evil threatened; but when the author lacks this right, the fear caused is unjust. Fear may proceed from some intrinsic cause, such as serious illness, or it may proceed from a cause extrinsic to the person suffering the fear.[5]

---

[1] Ayrinhac, *General Legislation*, p. 220; D. IV, 2, §2.

[2] *De Principiis*, n. 57.

[3] Can. 103 §1.

[4] Ayrinhac, *General Legislation*, p. 220; D. IV, 2, 1.

[5] Noldin, *De Principiis*, n. 55; Maroto, *Institutiones*, I, 460–461; Aryinhac, *General Legislation*, 220–221.

Canonists differ greatly in establishing the kind of fear that will invalidate religious profession. Some are of the opinion that any kind of fear, be it just or unjust, intrinsic or extrinsic, will be sufficient to cause a profession to be invalid. This is the teaching of Fanfani,[1] and Cocchi.[2] Schaefer[3] and Vermeersch-Creusen[4] hold that the fear must proceed from an extrinsic cause, but state that both just and unjust extrinsic fear are to be understood in connection with the present canon. The majority of canonists, however, rightly limit the canon to include only extrinsic, unjustly inflicted fear. This view is held by such authorities as Cappello,[5] De Meester,[6] Wernz-Vidal,[7] Maroto,[8] Papi,[9] Pejska,[10] Noldin,[11] and Oesterle.[12] The opponents of this view argue that the Code in canon 572, §1 4°, states without limitations that the profession must be made *sine metu*. From this they conclude that the legislator includes both just and unjust fear because, they say, "*ubi lex non distinguit, neque nos distinguere debemus.*" It is true enough that the canon makes no distinction between just and unjust fear, but as Cappello[13] and Oesterle[14] remark, there is no necessity for such a distinction, because no fear, inflicted to cause another to make profession against his will, can be just fear. Who can conceive an instance where a person has a right to force, by threats, another to take the vows of religion? To embrace the religious state is, of its very nature, a very personal affair; so much so that no one can claim a right to dictate whether or not another is to embrace that state. Hence for all practical purposes, justly inflicted fear is altogether foreign to this question.

---

1 *De Jure Religiosorum*, pp. 271–272.
2 *Commentarium*, lib. II, pars. IV, n. 77.
3 *De Religiosis*, p. 332.
4 *Epitome*, I, 390–391.
5 *Summa*, *J.C.* II, n. 599.
6 *Compendium*, II, 448, Fn. 2.
7 *De Personis*, p. 39.
8 *Institutiones*, I, 462.
9 *Religious in Church Law*, pp. 177, 271.
10 *Jus Canonicum Religiosorum*, p. 106.
11 *De Principiis*, n. 56, c.
12 *Jus Pontificium*, X (1930), 250.
13 *Summa J. C.*, II, n. 599.
14 *Jus Pontificium*, X (1930), 250.

A further argument that, in the interpretation of canon 572 §1, 4°, only extrinsic, unjust fear is to be understood, may be taken from canon 103 §2, which lays down the general rules for treating acts performed under the influence of fear. It states: *Actus positi ex metu gravi et injuste incusso...valent nisi aliud in jure caveatur.* The legislator here refers only to one kind of fear, namely, *unjust* fear, inflicted by an *extrinsic agent*, and states, furthermore, that ordinarily such fear will not invalidate an act, unless the law provides otherwise. Now, in canon 572 §1 4°, such a particular provision of law is made; it is one of the specific cases for which the legislator purposely departs from the general norm of canon 103 §2; in other words, it is one of the instances referred to by the legislator when, in canon 103, §2, he says: *Nisi aliud in jure caveatur.* Therefore it will be logical to conclude that canon 572 §1, 4°, is to be interpreted, not independently, but conjointly with canon 103 §2. Consequently, when canon 572 §1, 4°, decrees that profession, made under the influence of fear, is invalid, the canon must be interpreted to mean not any kind of fear, but fear as spoken of in canon 103 §2, which is fear unjustly inflicted by an extrinsic agent.

Moreover, in declaring profession, made under influence of fear, to be invalid, the Code merely restates the former legislation.[1] This being the case, the present law must be interpreted according to pre-Code canonists.[2] On the point in question, canonists before the Code, commonly taught that grave fear, unjustly inflicted by an extrinsic cause, was necessary to invalidate profession.[3] Consequently their opinion must be followed for interpreting the present legislation, so that also after the Code, only grave fear, *injuste incusso ab extrinseco,* will invalidate religious profession.

To guard against any violation of freedom of action in the matter of religious profession, a penalty of excommunication,

---

[1] Cf. for instance, c. 1, X, *de his, quæ vi metuve causa fiunt,* I, 40.

[2] "Canones quæ jus vetus ex integro referunt, ex veteris juris auctoritate, atque ex receptis apud probatos auctores interpretantibus, sunt æstimandi." —Can. 6, 2°.

[3] Cf. Bouix, *De Religiosis,* pars. IV, sec. 2, cap. n. 1; Reiffenstuel, *Jus canonicum Universum,* lib. III, tit. XXXI, n. 162; Makee, *Institutiones,* I, 493; Suarez, *De Statu Religionis et Perfectionis,* tract. VII, lib. IV, cap. IV, n. 11; Piat, *Prælectiones Juris Regularis,* I, 140.

reserved to no one, has been decreed against any person who will in any way force another to enter religious life or to make profession.[1] This excommunication is not, however, incurred until the person thus forced has either entered the novitiate, or has actually made profession.[2]

3. *Dolus*, or deceit, is any "connivance to cheat or to deceive another."[3] It may be committed by hiding the truth, by a deliberate lie, or by any other device, either in word or deed. Any act, therefore, either on the part of the religious superior or community, or on the part of the candidate for profession, which would cause the other party to enter into the contract of profession because deceived as to the true status of the matter, will invalidate the profession thus made. Thus Fanfani says, that if the true effects and obligations assumed by profession were deliberately concealed from the candidate who then makes profession with false notions of religious profession, that profession would be invalid, because of deceit.[4]

If the candidate himself is the perpetrator of the deceit, on account of which his profession is declared invalid, he will be expelled from the clerical state, if in minor orders; if he has already been promoted to major orders, he will be under suspension for as long a time as the Holy See sees fit.[5] This penalty, it must be noted, is not incurred by the very fact that the deceit has been committed; it will not be effective until the profession has been declared invalid.[6]

The Exploratio Voluntatis

To safeguard in a particular manner the liberty of women in embracing the life of the cloister, the Council of Trent originated the so-called *Exploratio Voluntatis*, or examination of the candidates. The Council decreed that before being admitted to the novitiate, and before making her profession, the candidate must be questioned by the bishop or a delegate, as to her motives for

[1] Can. 2352.
[2] Cappello, *De Censuris*, p. 364.
[3] Augustine, *Commentary*, II, 32.
[4] *De Jure Religiosorum*, p. 272.
[5] Can. 2387.
[6] Cappello, *De Censurius*, p. 467.

choosing the religious life, as to her knowledge of the obligations and duties imposed by this life, and as to her freedom of choice.[1]

Pope Leo XIII, in his constitution "*Conditæ a Christo*" of December 8, 1900,[2] extends the prescriptions to all religious orders and congregations of women. These prescriptions are retained by the Code and are set forth in canon 552. This canon directs that the superioresses of both exempt and non-exempt communities must inform the local Ordinary at least two months in advance of the date set for any investiture or profession, so that he or his delegate may be enabled to conduct the prescribed examination at least thirty days before the investiture or profession is to take place. A superioress who culpably fails to impart this information to the bishop in due time, is to be punished according to the gravity of the fault and, if the case warrants it, this punishment may be removal from office.[3] The *exploratio voluntatis*, according to the present legislation, is to take place before the admission to the novitiate, and before both temporary and perpetual profession, whether the latter be simple, or solemn. It is to take place only before the first and before the perpetual profession; hence in institutes where the making of annual profession is prescribed, this examination need not be repeated before each renewal of profession since, as Kinane remarks, this examination is to take place only "at the beginning of distinct stages of religious life."[4] Nor need it be held when for any reason the temporary profession is renewed before the perpetual profession actually takes place.[5] In no case, however, is this examination required for the validity of either the novitiate or the subsequent profession.

---

[1] "Libertati professionis virginum Deo dicandarum prospiciens sancta Synodus, statuit, atque decernit, ut puella, quæ habitum regularem suscipere voluit. . .non ante eum suscipiat, nec postea ipsa, vel alia professionem emittat, quam exploraverit episcopus, vel eo absente, vel impedito, ejus vicarius, aut aliquis eorum sumptibus ab eis deputatus, virginis voluntatem diligenter an coacta sit, an seducta sit, an sciat, quid agat; et si voluntas ejus pia, ac libera cognita fuerit, habueritque conditiones requisitas juxta monasterii illius, et Ordinis regulam, necnon monasterium fuerit idoneum."—Sess. XXV, *de regu-et monial.*, cap. XVII.

[2] *Fontes*, n. 644.

[3] Can. 2412 §2.

[4] *IER*, XVII (1921), 527.

[5] Schaefer, *De Religiosis*, p. 340.

§5 Express Profession

The Code demands that for the validity of the act, profession must be express.[1] Profession is express when in making it, such words or signs are employed which, of their very nature, serve unquestionably to manifest the will and intention of the person who makes use of them. Profession, therefore, to be express, may be made orally, it may be in writing, or it may take place by means of any perceptible signs, so long as these of their nature are expressive of the candidate's intent—so long as they will clearly manifest that the person who employs them is *hic et nunc*, actually making religious profession.[2] The constitutions of the various institutes must in every instance prescribe just how the candidate is to make his profession. What the constitutions prescribe for a valid express profession must be strictly complied with. It is a very common practice that in making his profession, the candidate write out and sign a prescribed formula of profession. The Code makes no provisions either concerning the formula in general, or as to what it must contain; these points are left to the constitutions to decide. Therefore, beyond the bare essentials, expressing the fact that the candidate by his act binds himself to the vows of religion, nothing more will be necessary as far as the general law is concerned. But for the completeness of the formula other points may be expressed. Although not necessary,[3] this formula may express the name of the superior who receives the profession; in case the superior acts through a delegate, the latter's name may then be mentioned.[4] In a general way, the vows of religion should also be mentioned.[5]

---

1 For the difference between express and tacit profession, and the final abolition of the latter as a valid method for making profession, see chapter II, art. 1, of this dissertation.

2 "Caput est ut quod Deo et religioni promittitur clare reddatur,"—Vermeersch-Creusen, *Epitome*, I, 423; cf. also Molitor, *Religiosi Juris Capita Selecta*, p. 147; Schmalzgrueber, *Jus Ecclesiasticum Universum*, tom. III, pars. IV, tit. XXXI, n. 179.

3 Vermeersch-Creusen, *Epitome*, I, 424.

4 "Formule des voeux"—*RCR*, IV (1928), 24; Augustine, *Commentary*, III, 257.

5 Leitner, *Handbuch*, III, 412; Augustine, *Commentary*, III, 265; Papi, *Religious in Church Law*, p. 270.

It is not, however, necessary that the vows be explicitly named.[1] Any clause or phrase which will implicitly include all the vows will be sufficient. Thus, for instance, the Benedictine professes "stability, conversion of morals, and obedience according to the rule;"[2] the Carthisian promises "conversion of morals according to the rule," while the reformed Cistercian uses the formula: "Father, I promise you obedience until death," to which the superior responds, "And I promise you life eternal."[3] It was only in the twelfth century that the practice of mentioning the three vows explicitly, arose. This custom was introduced by the founder of the Knights Templar, about the year 1119 or 1120; from the Knights Templar it passed over to the other military orders. It was then taken up by the later founders of religious orders, the first among whom was St. Francis of Assisi.[4] Another item which should be expressed in the formula of profession is the duration of the vows: the formula should mention whether the profession is to be obligatory for one year, for three years, or for life, as the case may be.[5] And, finally, the formula should state the nature of the profession—whether it is solemn or simple.

In prescribing that the profession must be express in order to be valid, the Code is satisfied with the mere general statement. The details as to what is to constitute an express profession are left to the constitutions of each institute to decide. Whatever these prescribe on this point must be strictly adhered to. But a departure from the prescriptions of the constitutions will not invalidate a profession, unless the constitutions expressly state that the prescriptions therein contained must be followed under pain of invalidating the act.

§6 Reception by Legitimate Superior

A final requirement for the validity of every religious profession, whether temporal or perpetual, simple or solemn, is that it be received by the legitimate superior. There is a difference

[1] Biederlack-Fuehrich, *De Religiosis*, p. 152; Vermeersch-Creusen, *Epitome*, I, 423; Piat, *Prælectiones Juris Regularis*, I, 144; Schaefer, *De Religiosis*, p. 332.

[2] *Regula S. P. N. Benedicti*, cap. 58.

[3] Cf. Vermeersch-Creusen, *Epitome*, I, 423.

[4] Scharnagl, *Das Feierliche Gelübde als Ehehinderniss*, p. 23.

[5] Leitner, *Handbuch*, III, 412; Augustine, *Commentary*, III, 256; Papi, *Religious in Church Law*, p. 276.

between admitting to profession and actually receiving the profession. The former, as explained above, in §2 of this chapter, signifies the giving of consent or permission to make profession. By admitting a novice to profession, the institute consents to enter into the profession contract; but by receiving the profession which it had authorized the candidate to make, that same institute, *de facto*, enters into the contract; it acccepts the *traditio* by means of which the candidate surrenders himself to the religious institute, and in return the institute obliges itself to provide and care for the neo-professed.[1] The fact that the religious institute actually enters into this contract with the candidate, must be manifested by means of some well determined external sign. This is accomplished when the properly appointed superior, in the name of the institute, receives and accepts the profession of the candidate.

The superior who receives the profession in the name of the institute must be one who is competent to represent the institute—he must be empowered so to act—otherwise the profession will be invalid. Like the admission to profession, so also the receiving of the profession is a part of the internal government. Consequently the right to receive the profession of candidates belongs, *per se*, to the religious superiors. The constitutions must in every case decide which superior is thus authorized to represent the institute for the reception of profession.[2] The superior thus authorized may, for just reasons, delegate his power to another. This power of delegation is likewise expressed in the present canon.[3]

To what extent is the local Ordinary to be considered a legitimate superior for receiving profession? As already remarked above, the act of receiving a profession is a part of the internal government of every religious institute, so that consequently, the right to receive professions of candidates belongs, *per se*, to the superiors in charge of the internal government, namely, to

[1] "Acceptatio...consensum in susceptionem professi sub speciali...potestate exprimit, simulque superiori hanc potestatem in personam professi, saltem in actu secundo confert;...est actus traditionem in Deum et voti emissionem extrinsice concomitans, quo ordinis superior servatis servandis consentit incorporationi eamque perficit..."—Molitor, *Religiosi Juris Capita Selecta*, p. 42.

[2] "...a legitimo superiore secundum constitutiones." Can. 572 §1, 6°.

[3] "...per se vel per alium." Can. 572 §1, 6°.

the major religious superiors. From a comparison between canons 572 §1, 6°, and 543, it would seem that both in the admission to, and in the reception of the professions of candidates, the major superiors alone are competent to act; the major superiors are those enumerated in canon 488, 8°. Now since, as already explained above in §2 of the present chapter, the enumeration of canon 488, 8° makes no mention of the local Ordinary, he is not, by general law, the legitimate superior to act in matters pertaining to profession. Canon 572 §1, 6°, does not, however, forbid the constitutions to authorize the bishop or his delegate to act instead of the major religious superior. The question then arises: when the constitutions do designate the ordinary to receive the professions, does the ordinary, in receiving the professions, act in his own name, or in the name of the religious superior? From what has just been said, it would be logical to conclude that in such cases the ordinary acts in the name of the superior as a delegate. This conclusion is certain in the case of religious women of pontifical right, as appears from the following response issued on March 1, 1921, by the Pontifical Commission for the Interpretation of the Code:

> **Cum in constitutionibus quarumdam congregationem religiosarum juris pontificii in formula professionis nulla fiat mentio antistitatae, sed tantummodo episcopi vel ejus delegati, quæritur:**
>
> **'An episcopus vel ejus delegatus in casu habendus sit legitimus Superior secundum Constitutiones ad professionem recipiendam, de quo in can. 572 §1, 6°.' Resp. Affirmative, tamquam habens legitimum mandatum.**[1]

Therefore, in the case submitted to the Commission, the Ordinary, in receiving the professions of these religious women of pontifical right, whose constitutions mention only the Ordinary as the superior for accepting professions, acts not in his own name, but in the name of the superioress; he acts as delegated by constitutions of the institute. The question immediately arises: may the conclusions of this response be applied also to institutes of diocesan right whose constitutions make similar provisions? An affirmative answer suggests itself because in all matters pertaining to the internal government, all religious institutes, whether

[1] Ad primum—*AAS*, XIII (1921), 177.

of pontifical or of diocesan right, are equally governed by the canons of the Code referring to religious. Since, therefore, the accepting of profession is part of the internal government of religious institutes, it is correct to conclude that the above response of the Pontifical Commission may also be applied to similar constitutionary laws of institutes of dioceasn right.

From the response of the Commission, cited above, it also follows that when, in similar cases, the constitutions do not expressly appoint the Ordinary or his delegate to receive the professions of candidates, and when, moreover, according to the constitutions, the professions are made directly into the hands of the superioress, the presence of the Ordinary or of his delegate is not required for the act. If in this latter case, the Ordinary is *de facto* present, he acts as a qualified witness to the profession.[1]

---

[1] Fanfani, *De Jure Religiosorum*, p. 273.

CHAPTER VI

TEMPORAL PROFESSION

Canon 574.

§1. In quilibet Ordine tam virorum quam mulierum et in qualibet Congregatione quæ vota perpetua habeat, novitius post expletum novitiatum, in ipsa novitiatus domo debet votis perpetuis, sive sollemnibus sive simplicibus, præmittere, salvo præscripto can. 634, votorum simplicium professionem ad triennium valituram, vel ad longius tempus, si ætas ad perpetuam professionem requisita longius distet, nisi constitutiones exigant annuales professiones.

§2. Hoc tempus legitimus Superior potest, renovata a religioso temporaria professione, prorogare, non tamen ultra aliud triennium.

Before the promulgation of the Code, temporal profession was practically unknown. It was the common opinion among pre-Code authorities, that perpetual profession was an essential element of the religious state.[1]

When Pius IX, in 1858, prescribed a period of simple profession as a prepapration for the making of solemn vows,[2] the perpetuity of religious profession remained intact; this is clearly evident from the decree "*Sanctissimus*," of 1858,[3] which gives an interpretation of the simple profession required by the encyclical "*Neminem Latet.*" This decree emphatically states that on the part of the religious, the vows are perpetual. The same is

---

[1] "...communiter Doctores docent ad statum religiosum constituendum cum votis simplicibus præter speciali S. Sedis indultum essentialiter requiri ut vota sint saltem ex parte voventis irrevocabilia...", S. C. Ep. et Reg. *Ordinis Hierosolymitani*, 27 Apr. 1866.—*Fontes*, n. 1997; cf. also Molitor, *Religiosi Juris Capita Selecta*, p. 12–24; Piat, *Prælectiones Juris Regularis*, I, 1; Goyeneche, "De Transitu ad aliam Religionem"—*CpR*, I (1920), 109–110; Larroana, *CpR*, II (1921), 208.

[2] Encycl. "*Neminem latet*"—Bizzarri, *Collect.*, p. 853.

[3] Bizzarri, *Collect.*, p. 855.

true of the simple vows prescribed for religious women by the decree "*Perpensis*," of 1902.[1] Even in the schema of the present Code, this opinion was adhered to. In the schema which appeared in 1912, it was stated that only in a broad sense could those be called religious who made only temporal profession.[2] It was only with the publication and promulgation of the final authentic edition of the Code that the name 'religious' was unrestrictedly applied also to the temporarily professed. But even here the characteristic note of perpetuity is preserved. The Code does not acknowledge a temporal profession, pure and simple, but requires a temporal profession which is to be renewed as each period expires.[3] To insure absolute continuity, the Code further prescribes that no space of time should be permitted to elapse between the expiration and renewal of the vows.[4] It is therefore the desire of the legislator that even temporal profession be made with the intention of renewing it at the proper time; with the intention, in other words, of persevering in the religious state until death. There is, however, no obligation imposed upon the religious to make this renewal when the period of temporal profession expires. Canon 575 §1, leaves the religious free either to renew his profession, or to return to secular life.[5]

§1 Its Necessity

The decree of Pius IX, "*Ad Universalis*,"[6] ordained that the simple profession prescribed by the earlier encyclical, "*Neminem Latet*,"[7] was required for the validity of the subsequent

---

[1] *ASS*, XXXV (1902–03), 31.

[2] "Extensive religionis vocabulum comprehendit quoque societatem, legitima auctoritate ecclesiastica approbatam, in qua tria illa vota nonnisi ad tempus nuncupantur."—Quoted from *CpR*, II (1921), 208, foot-note 77.

[3] Can. 488, 1°.

[4] "Elapso tempore ad quod vota sunt nuncupata, renovationi votorum nulla est interponenda mora."—Can. 577 §1.

[5] "Videtur ergo ad rationem status religiosi sec. mentem Ecclesiæ sufficere, ut obligatio stricta quidem ad tempus tantum contrahatur, intentio tamen tum voventis, tum religionis adsit, ut sodales in perpetuum in religione maneant, ita ut egressus per non renovationem votorum semper exceptionem importat."—Biederlack-Fuehrich, *De Religiosis*, p. 14, fn. 2.

[6] *Fontes*, n. 532.

[7] Bizzarri, *Collect.*, p. 853.

solemn profession; that solemn profession would be without any effect whatsoever if it had not been preceded by the required period of simple profession. The Code makes the same provision for temporal profession. In canon 572 §2, it is stated that for the validity of any perpetual profession, be it solemn or simple, it will be absolutely necessary that a period of temporal profession precede it.[1] The obligation to make temporal profession is further expressed in canon 574, quoted at the beginning of this chapter, in the words *novitius debet votis perpetuis præmittere*, etc. The verb *debet*, evidently imposes strict obligation, so that in case of failure to comply with this obligation, all future acts depending upon this present obligation will be null and void. Canon 574, however, has a further effect. Should a novice, contrary to the dictates of this canon, be nevertheless permitted to make perpetual profession immediately after his novitiate, not only will any future acts be null and void, but his present profession will likewise be invalid—a juridical non-entity—entailing absolutely no obligations, either in conscience or in the external forum; it will produce none of the effects which would otherwise follow the making of profession.[2]

The prescription of canon 574 §1, requiring preparatory temporal profession, is obligatory for all orders and congregations whose members are advanced to perpetual profession, whether the latter be solemn or simple. However, in applying the obligation, the word *perpetual* must be interpreted in its strictest sense to signify a profession which, with the possible exception of a dispensation, will continue until death. Profession which has this quality only conditionally is not to be included in applying this canon. Such a conditional profession would be one made with the proviso, "As long as I remain in the Congregation." Congregations whose members make profession with this, or similar conditions in reference to the duration of the vows are therefore not under the prescriptions of this canon and, consequently, have no obligation of making this preparatory temporal profession. This was expressly declared by the Pontifical Com-

---

[1] "Ad validitatem vero professionis perpetuæ sive solemnis sive simplicis, requiritur ut præcesserit professio simplex temporaria ad normam can. 574." —Can. 572 §2.

[2] Cf. S. C. de Rel., 30 Jul. 1909.—*AAS*, I (1909), 699.

mission for the Interpretation of the Code, in a response published March 1, 1921.[1]

Canon 574 makes another exception in favor of those professed religious who, with the proper permission, transfer to another order or congregation, according to the regulations of canon 634. These, *servatis servandis*, are to be admitted to perpetual profession in the institute to which they transfer, immediately after they have completed the required year of novitiate in the second institute.

§2 In Ipsa Novitiatus Domo

The phrase of canon 574 §1, *in ipsa novitiatis domo*, has given rise to much discussion as to its obligatory force. The question is: must temporal profession be made in the novitiate house under pain of invalidating the profession, or is it required only that the act may be licit?

With the view of solving this difficulty, it will be logical to appeal, in the first place, to pre-Code legislation. Here it is found that Clement VIII, on March 12, 1596, issued for Italy and the adjacent islands the decree "*Regularis Disciplinæ*,"[2] in which he declared that no one, under any pretext, could be received as a novice, or admitted to profession, except in a monastery approved by the Holy See; failure to comply with the dictates of the decree would render null and void any future reception of profession. A few years later, on June 20, 1599, he renewed the prescriptions of this decree by another decree, "*Sanctissimus*," but excepted a number of convents from its obligatory force.[3] Again on July 25, 1599, in the decree "*Nullus Omnino*,"[4] issued for the Servites, the same Pontiff prohibited the reception and profession of candidates in any but approved

---

[1] "In quibusdam institutis votorum simplicium vota emittuntur sub hac vel simili conditione apposita: 'donec in Congregatione vivam'; ita ut alumnus sive sponte discedat sive a Superioribus dimittatur, ipso facto a votis liber evadat. Hinc quæritur: In hisce institutis debente tali professioni præmitti triennium votorum temporariorum, ad normam c. 574?" Resp. "Negative." —*AAS*, XIII (1921), 178.

[2] *Fontes*, n. 183.

[3] *Fontes*, n. 181.

[4] *Fontes*, n. 187.

monasteries. These decrees of Clement VIII were later on confirmed by Urban VIII,[1] and by the Congregation of Bishops and Regulars in its instruction, *Florentina* of May 30, 1626.[2] These decrees, however, were all particular, in so far as they were addressed only to religious orders in Italy and the neighboring islands, and hence authorities generally, before the Code, taught that they were not obligatory outside of the territory for which they were issued, and that consequently what they prescribed for the novitiate and profession was not binding under pain of invalidity, except in territory expressly mentioned in the decrees.[3] The Congregation of Bishops and Regulars, on September 19, 1686, declared invalid the novitiate and professions of certain religious, which had not been made in accordance with the above named decrees.[4] This, like the decrees it refers to, had none but local bearing.

From the decrees cited, and from the opinions of authorities, it appears that, except in those particular localities mentioned in the decrees, the circumstance of place was, before the Code, not required for the validity of profession. Does the Code, in canon 574, depart from the pre-Code legislation to demand profession *in ipsa novitiatus domo* for validity of the act? That the circumstance of place is now required for the validity of every novitiate cannot be gainsaid. Canon 555 §1, 3°, is too plain in stating that for a valid novitiate it is required that, among other restrictions, *it be made in domo novitiatus.* It would seem that if the legislator had intended to make the same restriction for the temporal profession, he would have made this equally plain by adding an invalidating clause to canon 574 §1. The lack of this clause has led many canonists to conclude that only for liceity, and not for validity, must the first profession be made in the novitiate house.[5]

---

[1] Cf. Decr. S. C. C., 21 Sept. 1624—*Bull. Rom.*, V, 5, 249.

[2] *Fontes*, n. 1724.

[3] Bouix, *De Religiosis*, I, 579; Piat, *Prælectiones Juris Regularis*, I, 110–115, 135–136; Bachofen, *Compendium Juris Regularium*, p. 88.

[4] *Ordinis Carmelitarum—Fontes*, n. 1815.

[5] This is the opinion of such canonists as Vermeersch-Creusen, *Epitome*, I, 424; Pejska, *Jus Canonicum Religiosorum*, p. 109; Chelodi, *Jus de Personis*, n. 272; Blat, *Commentarium*, II, 556; Schaefer, *De Religiosis*, p. 336; Munerati, *Elementa J. C.*, p. 218, fn. 3; De Meester, *Compendium*, II, 448, fn. 6; Cance,

If canon 574 alone would have to be considered, this conclusion would be quite probable. But in deciding this point, is it sufficient to consider canon 574 §1, alone? Has canon 572 §2, no bearing on it? Canon 572 §2, demands that for the validity of perpetual profession, it must be preceded by a period of temporal profession, made *ad normam* c. 574. It demands, in other words, that in order validly to make perpetual profession, the requirements of canon 574 §1, be first complied with in the preparatory temporal profession. This latter canon prescribes three points: 1. that (except for the case mentioned in the canon) temporal profession must always precede perpetual profession; 2. that it be of at least three years' duration; and 3. that it be made in the novitiate house. Now, if perpetual profession, for its validity, is dependent upon the prescriptions of canon 574 having been fulfilled for the preparatory temporal profession, it would seem that, should any one of these points have been neglected in the making of temporal profession, the subsequent perpetual profession would not be valid, because temporal profession *ad normam* c. 574, had not preceded it. Consequently, to particularize, if in a given case, temporal profession was not made in the novitiate house, that profession was not made *ad normam* c. 574 and, therefore cannot fulfill the requirement of canon 572 §2, for the validity of the subsequent perpetual profession. Therefore, when canon 574 is interpreted, as it needs must be, in the light of canon 572 §2, all the points of canon 574 §1, collectively and severally, are required for validity.[1] Nor is the conclusion at variance with canon 11, which states:

Irritantes aut inhabilitantes, eae tantum leges habendæ sunt quibus aut actum esse nullum aut inhabilem esse personam, expressæ vel æquivalentes statuitur.

The nullifying or inhabilitating effect of a law may be either explicitly or implicitly expressed. It is explicitly expressed when

---

Le Code, II, 92; *Periodica*, XVI (1927), 161; Woywod, *HPR*, XXVII (1926), 188–189; Glaser, *LQS*, 83 (1930), 363–366. Goyeneche, *CpR*, VII (1926), 41, 185–186, though giving no definite answer is inclined to hold the opposite view; he says: "prima professio debet fieri—valde probabile ut valeat—in ipsa novitiatus domo, non in alia."

[1] Toso, *Commentaria Minora*, 140–141.

the import of the canon is quite evident; it is implicitly expressed when, though not self-evident, the nullifying or inhabilitating effect may nevertheless be shown to exist.[1] Canon 574 §1, when interpreted in the light of canon 572 §2, is just such a case in which the nullifying effect of the law is implicitly expressed. Consequently, when canon 572 §2, demands for the validity of perpetual profession, that temporal profession, made *ad normam canonis* 574, precede the making of perpetual profession, canon 572 §2, implicitly declares that the points enumerated in canon 574 §1, must be complied with for the validity of the act; and since the clause *in ipsa novitiatus domo* is one of these points contained in canon 574 §1, it likewise falls under the implicitly expressed nullifying effect contained in canon 572 §2. Therefore it is necessary for the validity of the temporal profession that it be made in the novitiate house.[2]

§3 Duration

Adhering to the former legislation for simple profession,[3] the Code establishes three years as the period required for the temporal profession. This is the general law for all religious institutes; without a papal Indult, no constitution may in general prescribe a longer period.[4] An exception from this general rule is made by the Code for those novices who, at the end of the three-year period, will not yet have reached the age required for perpetual profession. Such novices will, at the end of their novitiate, make, not triennial profession, but will make profession for the *entire* period which must elapse until they may validly be admitted to perpetual profession. Any novice, therefore, who at the end of his novitiate has not yet completed his eighteenth year, must make temporal profession, "until I have completed the

---

[1] "Implicita, seu in plico verborum, rei connexæ irritationem explicitam exprimentium, abscondita, revera tamen tamquam conclusio in principio, effectus in causa, minus in majore etc. ibi contenta, et per aperitionem verborum facile manifestabilis...", Michiels, *Normæ Generales*, I, 275.

[2] This view is held also by Toso, *Commentaria Minora*, p. 140–141.

[3] Cf. Encycl. "*Neminem latet*"—Bizzarri, *Collect.*, p. 853, and decr. "*Perpensis*," *ASS*, XXXV, 31.

[4] "Duree des Voeux Temporaires," *RCR*, VI (1930), 32; Papi, *Religious in Church Law*, p. 273.

twenty-first year of my age," or with some similar condition.[1] Another exception made by the Code, is for those institutes which prescribe annual profession before admitting candidates to perpetual profession. In such institutes the annual profession must be renewed each year for three years, or until the age required for perpetual profession has been attained.

The temporal profession must extend over a period of at least three complete years. In computing this period, the former legislation demanded an exact, mathematically complete, period extending from the moment of the first profession, until the re-occurrence of the same moment three years later. Solemn profession was declared to be invalid if made before the preparatory period of simple profession had been absolutely completed.[2] The Code no longer demands this strict computation *a momento ad momentum*. In computing the three-year period, according to the present legislation, the directions of canon 34 §3, 5°,[3] must be followed. Consequently, the term of triennial profession is completed on the third anniversary day of the first profession. The perpetual profession, being an *actus ejusdam generis*, may be made at any time during that anniversary day, regardless of the hour or moment of the day at which the first profession took place. Hence a religious who makes temporal profession on January 1, 1930, at two o'clock in the afternoon, all things being equal, may make perpetual profession at any time, morning or afternoon, on January 1, 1933. A slight exception to this rule of computation must be made if it should happen that the temporal profession is made on the 29th of February of a leap year. In such a case, the perpetual profession is to be made three years later, on February 28th, in accordance with canon 34 §3, 4°.[4]

---

[1] Vermeersch-Creusen, *Epitome*, I, 424; Chelodi, *Jus de Personis*, n. 272; Raus, *Institutiones*, p. 305; Blat, II, 556; Cappello, *Summa J. C.*, II, n. 611; Pejska, *Jus Canonicum Religiosorum*, p. 108; Jansen, *Ordensrecht*, p. 123; Brandys, *Kirchliches Rechtsbuch*, p. 42; Papi, *Religious in Church Law*, p. 273.

[2] On January 8, 1886, a sanation for a solemn profession, invalid because it had been made one hour too soon, was granted by the Holy See. *An. Juris Pont.*, XXVI, 376.

[3] "Si agatur de actibus ejusdem generis statis temporibus renovandis,... tempus finitur recurrente die quo incepit, sed novus actus per integrum eundem diem poni potest."—Can. 34 §3, 5°.

[4] "Quod si mensis die ejusdem numeri careat ... tunc pro diverso casu tempus finiatur incipiente vel expleto ultimo die mensis." Can. 34 §3, 4°.

In connection with this point, Vermeersch-Creusen[1] hold that the same rule of computation must be applied if at the end of his temporal profession, the religious decides to return to the world. According to these authors, a religious who made his temporal profession on January 1, 1930, may leave the monastery at any time on January 1, 1933, the day his vows expire. This, however, does not seem to be the correct conclusion. The norm just described is to be followed only when there is question of a renewal of an act of the same nature (*ejusdem generis.*) If the religious decides to leave the religious state at the completion of his temporal profession, there can be no question of an act of the same nature; in consequence, not number 5, but number 3, of canon 34 must be followed, which states that the time is completed at the close of the recurring anniversary day, so that the religious in question is not free to leave until the morning of January 2, 1933.[2]

§4 Prorogation

The second paragrpah of canon 574 authorizes the proper superior to prolong the period of temporal profession, but not beyond another three-year term. The legitimate superior who may prolong the term of temporal profession is the major superior who, according to the constitutions of the institute, is empowered to admit candidates to profession.[3] Neither the advice nor the consent of the chapter is necessary to make this prolongation, since canon 574 §2, makes no reference to this effect; it states simply "*legitimus superior potest,*" etc. Canon 575 §2, is likewise silent on this point; it prescribes the vote of the chapter only for the first and for the perpetual profession.[4] In order to prolong the profession, the superior must, however, have a sufficient reason for so acting.

---

1 *Epitome*, I, 427; cf. also Schaefer, *De Religiosis*, p. 340.

2 Schweigman, "De duratione validitatis professionis temporariæ,"—*Nederlandsche Katholieke Stemmen*, 1929, p. 148.

3 Pruemmer, *Manuale J. C.*, q. 214, fn. 9; Vermeersch-Creusen, *Epitome*, I, 425; Papi, *Religious Profession*, p. 24; Augustine, *Commentary*, III, 261; Goyeneche, *CpR*, IV (1923), 52.

4 Fanfani, *De Jure Religiosorum*, pp. 275–276; Papi, *Religious in Church Law*, p. 274.

The temporal profession may be prolonged for a period not exceeding three years. It is immaterial whether this period is continuous, or is made for succeeding intervals of, for instance, six months or one year.[1] No matter for how long a period the profession has been prolonged, it is not necessary to await the completion of the extended period in order to admit such a religious to his perpetual profession. Just as soon as the cause for the prolongation has ceased, or just as soon as the religious in question is found fit, he may be admitted to perpetual profession, irrespective of how much of the extended period has elapsed.[2]

A difficulty arises in interpreting the expression *hoc tempus*. Does it refer to the phrase *ad triennium*, or does it include also the clause *ad longius tempus*, of the first paragraph of canon 574? If the former be true, then no more than six years could be spent in temporal profession. But if the latter can be held, then temporal profession of five years, made because the novice was only sixteen years of age at the time of his first profession, could be prolonged for another three years. Authors disagree in their interpretation. Some[3] hold that *hoc tempus* is to be applied either to the *ad triennium*, or to the *longius tempus*, as the case may be. Other authorities,[4] on the contrary, consider *hoc tempus* applicable only to the *ad triennium*, so that it would be beyond the intent of the canon to prolong the profession in such a way that it would comprise more than six years. It is rather difficult to give a definite decision in the matter. Both opinions have reasons to support them. But considering the canon as it stands, the first view rests on the more solid foundation. The period (*hoc tempus*) which the superior may prolong, is the same as the period stated in the first paragraph of canon 574. It is there stated that the temporal profession is to extend over a term

---

[1] Goyeneche, *CpR*, V (1924), 441–442; Papi, *Religious in Church Law*, p. 275. Blat, however, *Commentarium*, II, 256–257, states that such a procedure is not permissible.

[2] Fanfani, *De Jure Religiosorum*, pp. 301–302; Jansen, *Ordensrecht*, p. 123; Schaefer, *De Religiosis*, p. 337.

[3] Fanfani, *De Jure Religiosorum*, p. 302; Augustine, *Commentary*, III, 260.

[4] Vermeersch-Creusen, *Epitome*, I, 426; Sipos, *Enchiridion J.C.*, p. 259, fn. 13; Pruemmer, *Manuale J. C.*, q. 214; De Meester, *Compendium*, II, 449, fn. 4; Jansen, *Ordensrecht*, p. 126; *Periodica*, XVI (1927), 160; "Prolongations des Voeux Temporaires,"—*RCR*, V (1929), 116.

of three years, *or longer*, if the age of the novice so requires. This being the case, there is nothing to forbid the superior to prolong the term made for three years, for an additional three years, if he sees fit. Nor does the phrase *non ultra alius triennium* militate against this conclusion. This limitation is to be interpreted to mean that the term of prolongation may not be more than three years in excess of the actual period for which the temporary profession was originally made.

§5 Renewal

Renewal of vows may be either *devotional* or *canonical.* The former, although not obligatory in virtue of any general legislation, may be prescribed by the various constitutions of religious institutes, in order to rekindle the religious spirit of its members. This devotional renewal of profession may take place even after the religious has made his perpetual vows. The Code makes no provisions for the devotional, but refers only to the canonical renewal. There are, in general, two instances when the canonical renewal of profession must be made, namely: 1. in communities whose members make annual profession; and 2. when for any reason the term of the temporal profession is prolonged by the legitimate superior in accordance with the prescriptions of canon 574 §2. The spirit of the Code, and the stability of the religious state demand that, once the first profession has been made, the religious ought never to be without vows. Hence if for any reason perpetual profession will not take place immediately after the period of temporal profession expires, even though only a single day would elapse between the expiration of the temporal and the making of perpetual profession, the temporary vows must be renewed for that space of time.[1] But, to omit this renewal of the temporary vows for the space of time that is to elapse between the expiration of the first profession and the making of perpetual profession, would be no more than an illicit procedure; the perpetual profession would not be invalid on that account.[2]

---

[1] Goyeneche, *CpR*, IV (1923), 51.

[2] Vermeersch-Creusen, *Epitome*, I, 427; Raus, *Institutiones*, p. 306; Cance, *Le Code*, II, 94; Goyeneche, *CpR*, VIII (1927), 33–34; *Periodica*, XV (1926), (29); *ibid*, XVI (1927), 160.

The canonical renewal of profession must take place just as soon as the term of the previous profession has expired.[1] To determine the day on which this renewal must take plcae, the prescriptions of canon 34 §3, 5°, as explained above in §4 of the present chapter, are to be applied. Accordingly, the renewal must be made on the anniversary day of the previous profession. On this point, the view taken by Augustine,[2] when he says: "the renewal must take place after the 365th day, or on the first day after the year is completed," cannot be followed. There is question here of an act *ejusdem generis*. Therefore, as canon 34 §3, 5° clearly states, when there is question of renewing such acts which partake of the same nature as the previous act, the renewal must take place on the anniversary day itself.

The renewal of the temporary vows may be anticipated, with the limitation, however, that it take place not more than one month in advance of the actual day on which the previous profession will expire.[3] The superior who is authorized to permit the anticipation, is the same one who is designated by the constitutions as the legitimate major superior for admitting candidates to profession.[4] In order to act licitly, the superior must have a just cause for permitting anticipation. A sufficient cause is present if the anticipation is permitted to take place so that a group of religious, who had made their previous profession on different days, may renew their vows at the same occasion.[5] In like manner, sickness, departure for a house of studies, and similar causes also constitute lawful reasons to warrant anticipating the renewal of profession.[6] Anticipation may take place only when there is question of the renewal of temporal profession. Under no circumstances may perpetual profession take place before the term of triennial profession has been completed, or before the

[1] "Elapso tempore ad quod vota sunt nuncupata, renovatione votorum nulla est interponenda mora."—Can. 577 §1.

[2] *Commentary*, III, 267.

[3] "Superioribus tamen facultas est ex justa causa permittendi ut renovatio votorum temporariorum per aliquod tempus, non tamen ultra mensem, anticipetur."—Can. 577 §2.

[4] Schaefer, *De Religiosis*, p. 340, fn. 4.

[5] De Meester, *Compendium*, II, n. 1006.

[6] Augustine, *Commentary*, III, 267.

temporarily professed has attained the age required for making perpetual profession.

The renewal of temporary vows must always be a public act. In making the renewal, all the requirements of canon 572 §1, for a valid profession must be complied with. Moreover the prescriptions of canon 576 §2, in reference to the proper recording of profession, should likewise be observed.[1]

---

[1] Fanfani, *De Jure Religiosorum*, p. 284; Schaefer, *De Religiosis*, p. 339; Goyeneche, *CpR*, IV (1923), 51; Woywod, *HPR*, XXX (1930), 1095.

CHAPTER VII

PERPETUAL PROFESSION

Canon 575, §1.

Exacto professionis temporariæ tempore, religiosus, ad normam can. 637, vel emittat perpetuam professionem, sollemnem vel simplicem secundum constitutiones, vel ad sæculum redeat; ...

ARTICLE 1

ADMISSION TO PERPETUAL PROFESSION

During the period which the religious spends in temporary vows, he must show by his conduct that he has the necessary qualifications of character which go to make a good religious; he must, at the same time, give evidence, by his observance of the regulations, that he is able, both mentally and physically, to assume, for the remainder of his life, the duties and obligations, the burdens and privations which the constitutions of the order or congregation to which he chooses to consecrate his entire self, imposes upon its members.

At the expiration of the term of his temporal profession, two alternatives are open to the religious: he may either return to the secular life of the world, or he may apply for admission to perpetual profession. Should he choose the former, he is free to leave the monastery as soon as his temporary vows have expired. Hence, according to the norms of canon 34 §3, 3°, he may leave on the morning following the anniversary day of his first profession.[1] In order to leave the monastery at the expiration of his temporal profession, the religious requires neither permission nor indult; he is absolutely free from all obligations.[2]

[1] For further explanation of this point see chapter VI, §3, of this dissertation.

[2] "Professus a votis temporariis, expleto votorum tempore, libere potest religionem deserere..."—Can. 637

Nor is he obliged to reimburse the religious community for any expenses he may have caused the community to incur during the time of his temporary vows.

Should the temporarily professed choose to remain a religious after the expiration of his temporary vows, he is obliged to apply for admission to perpetual profession. Whether or not he will be admitted will depend entirely upon the decision of the religious superior, after the latter has obtained the advice of the chapter or council.[1] If the candidate is considered to be unsuited for the religious life of the cloister, the superior has a right to deny the religious admission to perpetual profession. But to do this, the superior must be actuated by just and grave reasons,[2] because temporal profession gives to the professed religious a claim to be advanced to perpetual profession at the proper time, unless for weighty causes it becomes evident that he is unqualified either for religious life in general, or for the duties and obligations which may be required of its members by a particular order or congregation. Among the causes which may be considered sufficiently grave to refuse admission to perpetual profession may be enumerated a lack of the true religious spirit; the existence of a deep-rooted, unconquerable evil habit; furthermore, when there is question of a clerical religious, a want of the necessary talent for progress in studies, or a continued failure, whether culpable or otherwise, in the important branches of the sacred sciences will be ample reason to deny to such a religious admission to perpetual profession.[3] But it must be remembered that if this inability for studies is the result of an illness contracted after his temporal profession, such a religious may *not* be refused admission to perpetual profession since, as will be seen immediately, illness is not a sufficient reason for debarring a temporarily professed from perpetual profession.[4]

Among the causes which do not constitute a sufficient reason for dropping a religious from the community by refusing him

---

[1] Can. 575 §2; see also Chapter V, §2, of this dissertation.

[2] "...pariter religio ob justas ac rationabiles causas eundem potest a renovandis votis temporariis vel ab emittenda professione perpetua excludere..." —Can. 637.

[3] Fanfani, *De Jure Religiosorum*, pp. 313, 480–481; Schaefer, *De Religiosis*, p. 562; Goyeneche, *CpR*, I (1920), 135–236, III (1922), 82–83.

[4] Fanfani, *De Jure Religiosorum*, p. 498–499.

admission to perpetual profession at the expiration of his temporary vows, is ill health, unless it can be conclusively proven that the malady existed, and was deliberately concealed or dissimulated by the novice when he applied for admission to temporary vows at the conclusion of his year of novitiate.[1] "A physician's testimony," says Augustine, "accompanied by an affidavit to the effect that the religious deceived the institution by his assertions, would be legal proof, as would also be the testimony of two witnesses in whose presence the religious, before his first profession, asserted that he was in good health, if it can be proved by a physician's sworn certificate that the illness existed before he entered; for in such a case, deceit or fraud is evident."[2] But if the novice, when applying for temporal profession, revealed his true physical weakness or disease, and the community, with full knowledge of the state of his health, nevertheless admitted him to temporal profession, the latter may not debar such a religious from making perpetual profession, even though his condition became more serious during the period of his temporary vows. So likewise, a religious who, during his temporal profession, contracts a disease, or who has had the misfortune to sustain a permanent bodily injury must, despite his present condition, be permitted to make perpetual profession, unless of his own free choice he prefers to return to secular life in the world.[3] It may be necessary, under certain conditions, that a religious spend a considerable period of time away from his monastery, due to the condition of his health. Even though in the meantime his temporary vows expire, he does not on that account forfeit his right to return, as long as he never expressed an intention of quitting the religious state. At his return he has a perfect right to be readmitted and to be advanced to perpetual profession.[4]

---

[1] "...religio pariter...eundem potest a renovandis votis temporariis vel ab emittenda professione perpetua excludere, non tamen ratione infirmitatis, nisi certo probetur eam ante professionem fuisse dolose reticitam aut dissimulatam."—Can. 637; cf. also S. C. Ep. et Reg., *Capuccinorum*, 10 Mart. 1650—*Fontes*, n. 1790; S. C. super Stat. Rel. 12 Jun. 1858—Bizzarri, *Collect.*, p. 855–857; S. C. Ep. et Reg., *Ordinis S. Benedicti*, 13 Maj. 1904.—*Fontes*, n. 2048; Toso, *Commentaria Minora*, p. 148.

[2] *Commentary*, III, 372.

[3] Woywod, *HPR*, XXVII (1921), 289–290.

[4] "Nullo canone sancitur ut extraneus fiat Instituto religiosus qui, elapso tempore, vota simpliciter non renovaverit vel in domo religioso non sit com-

It may happen that the affliction which befalls a religious is of such a nature as to render the making of perpetual profession impossible. This is particularly the case with those who become insane. What is their status at the end of their temporal profession? Who is to provide for them? These questions were proposed to the Sacred Congregation of Religious, to which it responded that such unfortunate religious continue to be members of their community. Even though they be unable to make perpetual profession, the community is not thereby released from its obligations to provide for them; the community must take care of their needs, just the same as it must for any other member.[1]

The temporarily professed religious who applies for admission to perpetual profession and is accepted, must be permitted to make his perpetual vows just as soon as the temporary vows have expired.[2] As already explained in the foregoing chapter, the perpetual profession may take place at any time during the day on which the term of preparatory temporal profession, as prescribed by canon 572 §2, expires, that is, on the anniversary day of the first profession. No delay is to take place between the expiration of the temporal and the making of perpetual profession. If for any reason the perpetual profession can not take place on the day on which the first vows expire, the latter must be renewed for the space of time that is to elapse until the perpetual profession will finally take place.

---

moratus,..."—Vermeersch, *Periodica*, XII (1923), (17); cf. also Piontek, *De Indulto Exclaustrationis necnon Sæcularisationis*, p. 158–159; *AER*, 69 (1923), 304.

[1] "I. Utrum professus votorum in Ordine vel in Congregatione, qui durante triennio amens evaserit, judicio medicorum etiam insanabiliter, possit, finito triennio, ad suos vel ad sæculum remitti, an vero debeat in Religione retineri; et quatenus negative ad primam partem, affirmative ad secundam; II. Qualis sit prædicti Religiosi conditio juridica, et ad quid teneatur religio in casu." "RESP. ad I. Negative ad primam partem, affirmative ad secundam; ad II. Religiosus de quo in dubio I, pertinet ad Religionem in eo statu in quo erat quando mente captus est, et Religio tenetur ad eadem officia ad quæ tunc tenebatur."—S. C. Rel., 5 Feb. 1925—*AAS*, XVII (1925), 107. See also Maroto, *CpR*, VI (1925), 170–179; *HPR*, XXVI (1926), 522–523.

[2] "Exacto professionis temporariæ tempore, religiosus...emittat perpetuam professionem...—Can. 575 §1; Elapso tempore ad quod vota sunt nuncupata, renovationi votorum nulla est interponenda mora."—Can. 577 §1.

For the validity of the perpetual profession, the general requirements for profession set down in canon 572 §1, must be strictly adhered to.[1] The prescriptions of canon 572 §2, demanding at least three complete years of preparatory temporal profession, as well as those of canon 573, demanding that the candidate for perpetual profession have completed the twenty-first year of his age, must likewise be minutely observed.

Article 2.

SOLEMN AND SIMPLE PROFESSION

Perpetual profession may be either solemn or simple.[2] That profession is solemn in which solemn vows are made; simple, in which simple vows are made.[3] Solemn vows, according to the Code, are those which are acknowledged by the Church to be solemn, while all other religious vows are simple vows only.[4]

§1 The Foundation of Solemnity

The religious who makes solemn vows, makes a perpetual contract by which he surrenders his entire self to the service of God and of His Church; this engagement the Church solemnly accepts. The religious, however, who makes perpetual simple vows, surrenders himself in the same manner; before God he takes upon himself the same obligations as does the one who makes solemn vows, but his engagement is not accepted by the Church in the same manner as is the engagement of the one who makes solemn vows.[5]

---

[1] See Chapter V for explanation of these points.

[2] Can. 575 §1.

[3] Fanfani, *De Jure Religiosorum*, p. 270.

[4] "Votum est sollemne, si ab Ecclesia uti tale fuerit agnitum; secus simplex." —Can. 1308 §2.

[5] "The Simple Vows of the Professed Religious in the U. S."—*AER*, XII (1895), 312; "Il y dans la profession religieuse un double engagement: l'un vis-à-vis de Dieu, l'autre vis-à-vis de l'Eglise. Mais deux tous dependent de l'Eglise...;D'où il résulte que les deux engagements ne sont ni plus stable, ni plus irrévocables que l'Eglise ne l'entend ..."—Mercier, "Les Voeux Solennels,"—*Rev. Thom.*, 27 (1922), 399.

When speaking of the solemnity connected with vows and profession, one must clearly distinguish between the accidental and the essential solemnity. Accidental solemnity consists in the external ceremonies and formalities accompanying the making of solemn profession; while the substantial solemnity consists in that essential quality without which profession cannot be solemn.

The question, therefore, naturally arises: what is that necessary and essential quality which, when present, renders a particular vow or profession solemn; and which, when absent, leaves a profession a simple one?—or in other words, what is the foundation for the solemnity of profession?

Various opinions and theories have, in the past, been advanced by canonists to solve the question. These various theories may be reduced to three general heads: 1. that the essential solemnity of a vow consists in, and is derived from, an external benediction or consecration; 2. that it consists in the *traditio*, or surrender of self; 3. that it consists in some extrinsic quality established by the authority of the Church.

a) *Theory of Consecration*

The first opinion holds that the solemnity of vows and of profession consists in, and is derived from, some benediction or consecration which accompanies the making of profession. This opinion seems to have been fostered by St. Thomas; he distinctly says: "*Solemnitas voti in quadam spirituali benedictione ac consecratione consistit.*"[1] The foundation upon which the patrons of this theory rest their conclusions is this: every external contract must be accompanied by some formalities or solemnities to give it legal force; since a vow is also a contract, it must likewise have some formality or solemnity to add obligatory force to it; because, furthermore, a vow is a contract made with God, its solemnity should consist in some sacred benediction or consecration.[2]

If this opinion be correct, it must needs follow that every vow, in order to be solemn, must be made with an accompanying benediction or consecration, since the essential solemnity of a

[1] *Secunda secundæ*, q. 88, a. 9.

[2] Suarez, *De Statu Perfectionis et Religionis*, lib. II, cap. 6, n. 2.

vow consists precisely in that essential quality without which a vow cannot be solemn. To admit that the substantial solemnity of a vow could consist in a quality which may either be present, or may be absent, would be to admit an absurdity. Historical facts show clearly that the making of vows was not always accompanied by a consecration or blessing, and yet, such vows have nevertheless been considered true solemn vows. This fact is evident from the history of profession. Throughout the Middle Ages, entrance into a religious order and solemn profession went hand in hand. Whosoever became a religious was *ipso facto* bound by solemn vows.[1] But, on the other hand, throughout that same period of time, tacit profession, made entirely without external formalities, unaccompanied by either blessing or consecration, was authoritatively held to be a valid means of profession.[2] The effects and obligations of tacit profession were identical with those imposed by express profession.[3] Since, therefore, by tacit profession, solemn vows could validly be made, it must then follow that the solemnity of vows cannot consist in any external consecration or blessing, because otherwise substantial, essential solemnity could consist in a quality which could be absent from the vow.

Again, if the solemnity of vows consists in a blessing or consecration, it must necessarily be true that, if the required consecration really takes place at the time the vows are made, those vows must of necessity be solemn, since, as is supposed, the substantial solemnity consists in that essential quality which, when present, causes the vows to be solemn. But there are cases in which vows are made with all the accompanying blessings prescribed by the ritual of some particular institute, and yet these vows may nevertheless be no more than simple vows. This fact is borne out by a decision of the Congregation of Bishops and Regulars, issued on the 21 of April, 1841. In a certain convent, in which solemn vows had always been made, the State usurped

---

[1] "Feierliche Gelübde und Entstehung des Ordenswesens" — *Stimmen aus Maria-Laach*, Ergbd., XVII, Heft 65, p. 24.

[2] C. 22, 23, X *de Regularibus*, III, 31; c. 3, *de Regularibus et transeuntibus ad religionem*, III, 14 in VI°; c. 2. *de Regularibus et transeuntibus ad religionem*, III, 9 in Clem.; Benedict XIV, const. "*Anno Vertente*," June 19, 1570—*Bull. de prop. Fide.*, III, 270.

[3] Schmalzgrueber, *Jus Eccles. Univ.*, pars. IV, tit. XXXI, n. 157.

the power of legislating in reference to the admission of candidates and the profession of novices. The laws of this particular government demanded that after the novice had reached the age of twenty-one years, she was to make *solemn triennial* vows; these were then to be renewed every three years, until the religious attained the age of thirty-three. Only then could the religious be permitted to make solemn perpetual profession. In making the so-called solemn triennial vows, the entire ritual, prescribed by the *Pontificale Romanum* for solemn profession was always followed. Doubts arose concerning these professions, and the matter was referred to the Holy See. The Congregation of Bishops and Regulars, on April 21, 1841, responded to the doubts proposed by stating that the vows in question were not solemn. In making these vows, all the blessings and ceremonies prescribed for solemn profession had been observed, and yet the vows made, were only simple. Blessings, therefore, as this case clearly shows, do not constitute the substantial solemnity of profession.[1]

b) *Traditio Theory*

The second opinion advanced toward the solution of the question teaches that the solemnity of profession consists in the *traditio*, or surrender of self, by which the novice gives himself over entirely to the religious order. Among others who held this opinion were Gregory of Valence.[2] and some of the disciples of St. Thomas.[3] The foundation upon which the exponents of this theory base their conclusion is this: a thing given to one person cannot validly be given to another (*res uni tradita non potest alteri valide donari...*).[4] The followers of this opinion distinguish between the vow, or promise made to God, on the one hand, and the surrender of self on the other.[5] Hence they argue that if a person makes a promise to give to a Church a particular valuable article, that person does not thereby give up the ownership or

---

[1] Cf. Bizzarri, *Collect.*, p. 463.

[2] Vermeersch, *De Religiosis*, II, (13); Ballay, "Quæstiones quædam de Votis Simplicibus, præsertim quæ votis solemnibus præmittuntur."—*AkKR*, 17 (1867), 19.

[3] Vermeersch, *op. cit.*, p. (13).

[4] Suarez, *De Statu Perfectionis et Religionis*, lib. II, cap. 7, n. 3.

[5] Bouix, *De Jure Regularium*, pars. I, sec. III, cap. 2, n. 3.

dominium of that article until he actually gives the article to the Church. By virtue of his promise he is bound to make the donation, but should he, after having made the promise, give the article to a third person, he would violate his promise, but his act would nevertheleess be valid. Carrying this idea into the realm of religious profession, the patrons of this opinion maintain that a person, who makes a vow of chastity, but in that vow does not include the surrender of self, would sin indeed by contracting a subsequent marriage, but his marriage would be valid. But, on the contrary, they continue, one who includes the surrender of self in his vow, gives the *dominium* of his own body to God, and therefore cannot contract a valid marriage, because what has been given to one person cannot validly be given to another. The one surrendering himself to God by a vow of chastity, cannot give himself validly to another in marriage. From this they conclude that the one who makes vows without including the surrender of self, makes only simple vows, while another who includes the surrender, makes solemn vows. Their final conclusion, therefore, is that the solemnity of vows is dependent upon, and consists in, this *traditio* or surrender of self.

The fundamental error of this theory is, that it admits the possibility of a religious vow or profession in which the *traditio* does not take place—a thing which cannot be admitted. The surrender of self, as pointed out elsewhere in this treatise,[1] is an essential element of every religious profession, be it solemn or only simple. That one become a religious, it is absolutely necessary that he cede his rights, and surrender himself bodily to the religious institute, a thing which can be accomplished only by means of the surrender of self.

To show further the fallacy of this opinion, various arguments can be advanced. In the first place, if the substantial, essential solemnity of vows and of profession is to be placed in the surrender of self, then every vow or profession in which this surrender takes places, must of necessity, be solemn, since the very notion of a substantial solemnity demands that if it be present, the vow will necessarily be a solemn one. But there exist vows in which the surrender actually takes place, but which vows, despite the surrender, remain only simple vows. A case in point

[1] Pages 5, 6.

is the vows made by Scholastics in the Society of Jesus. Gregory XIII, in the constitution "*Ascendente Domino,*" of May 25, 1584,[1] calls these vows of the Jesuits "*vota substantialia;*" he moreover states expressly that all who make vows in the Society are "*vere et proprie religiosi;*" therefore the surrender actually takes place, because, as pointed out above, this surrender is an essential element of every religious vow and profession. But despite the surrender of self, the vows of the Jesuit Scholastics are not solemn, but simple, a fact which was clearly shown by Gregory XIII, in the constitution "*Ascendente Domino.*"[2] Hence it follows, as a necessary conclusion that, if vows may be simple, even though the surrender of self has taken place, this surrender of self cannot constitute the substantial solemnity of vows or of profession.

The surrender of self belongs to the very nature and essence of every religious profession. If therefore, the solemnity of profession consists in the surrender of self, it would follow that the solemnity of profession is a factor inherent in the very nature of profession and that, in consequence, this solemnity is of natural or of divine origin.[3] This, however, is contrary to the teaching of several Popes, who clearly assert that the solemnity of profession is of ecclesiastical origin. The words of Boniface VIII, on the matter, cannot be mistaken.[4] The statement of Boniface VIII is repeated verbatim by Gregory XIII, in his constitutions "*Quanto fructuosius,*" of February 1, 1583,[5] and "*Ascendente Domino,*" of May 25, 1854.[6] That the solemnity of profession is of ecclesiastical institution is likewise implicitly declared in a decision of the Congregation of Bishops and Regulars, issued on September 1, 1854.[7] In a certain city of Italy there existed a convent of nuns whose institution was one in which the making of

---

1 *Fontes,* n. 153.

2 "...statutum est ut novitii in Societate...tria...vota simplicia emittunt..."—*loc. cit.*

3 Suarez, *De Statu Perfectionis et Religionis,* lib. II, cap. 8, n. 1; Bouix, *De Jure Regularium,* pars. I, sec. III, cap. 1, n. 3.

4 "...Voti solemnitas ex sola constitutione ecclesiæ est inventa..."—cap. unic., *de Voto et Voti Redemptione,* III, 15 in VI°.

5 *Fontes,* n. 150.

6 *Fontes,* n. 153.

7 Bizzarri, *Collect.,* p. 634.

solemn profession was prescribed. When the convent in question had been erected, the consent of the Holy See, as required by Innocent III,[1] Gregory X,[2] and John XXII,[3] had not been obtained. A doubt, therefore, arose in the mind of the Superioress whether or not the vows made by the nuns were really solemn. The Congregation responded in the negative,[4] because of the lack of canonical erection, showing thereby that solemnity of vows is entirely dependent on the legislation of the Holy See, which would not be the case, were the solemnity of divine origin.

c) *Theory of Ecclesiastical Institution*

From what has thus far been said concerning the solemnity of religious profession, it is evident that neither the opinion, placing this solemnity in a consecration, nor the other, considering the *traditio* to be the foundation of solemnity, can be retained. There can be but one solution to the question—that which places this solemnity solely in the institution of the Church. The foundation for this solution rests in the positive utterances of several Popes. Boniface VIII was the first to declare positively this fact when he said that the solemnity is: "*ab ecclesia inventa...*"[5] The very same words were later repeated by Gregory XIII.[6]

§2 The Essential Difference Between Solemn and Simple Profession

From what has gone before, the question will naturally suggest itself: What is the specific difference which exists between the solemn and simple vow, and in consequence also between the solemn and simple profession? As a result of the special recognition on the part of the Church, some extrinsic quality is added to the solemn vow, which is lacking in the simple vow. In-

---

[1] C. 9, X, *de Religiosis Domibus ut Episcopo sint subjectæ*, III, 36.

[2] Cap. Unic., *De Religiosis Domibus*, III, 17, in VI°.

[3] Cap. unic., *De Religiosis Domibus*, tit. VII, in Extrav. Joan. XXII.

[4] "...ad dubium: 'Se a come respondere alla instanza della Superiora del Monastero...nel case'; Rescripsimus: Pro sanatione erectionis Monasterii... et pro sanatione in radice votorum emissorum..."—S. C. Ep. et Reg., Sept. 1, 1854, Bizzarri—*Collect.*, p. 634.

[5] Cap. unic., *De Voto et Voti Redemptione*, III, 15, in VI°.

[6] Const. "*Quanto Fructuosis*," Feb. 1583 1—*Fontes*, n. 150; Const. "*Ascendente Domino*," 25 Maj. 1584.—*Fontes*, n. 153.

trinsically, there is no difference between the solemn and the simple vow. "A solemn vow and a simple vow are one in the essential idea of a vow. Every vow, whether simple or solemn, induces an obligation of religion in virtue of a promise which has thereby been made to God. Transgression of either simple or solemn vows is essentially of the same kind of wickedness."[1] The obligations which the simply professed religious takes upon himself are, intrinsically, the same as those assumed by the religious who makes solemn profession; both solemn and simple profession include the surrender of the entire person of the religious to the religious order or congregation for which the profession is made. The difference between the solemn and simple profession must, therefore, be an extrinsic one. In virtue of the special recognition which the solemn profession receives from the Church,[2] some extrinsic quality is added to the solemn vow; this quality is the power of invalidating certain acts which are performed contrary to the vow.[3] For want of this superadded quality acts performed contrary to simple vows are only illicit. The essential difference, therefore, between the solemn and the simple profession consists in the fact that they produce different effects. It is, however, necessary that one distinguish clearly between the *power* of invalidating, in the case of solemn profession, or of rendering only illicit, in the case of simple vows, certain acts contrary to the vows; and the *result of this power*, or the fact that such contrary acts are *de facto* either invalid or illicit, as the case may be. The difference between the solemn and the simple profession lies in the respective *power* of either invalidating or rendering illicit contrary acts, not in the fact that these acts are *de facto* either invalid or illicit, as the case may be.

This difference between the solemn and simple profession is best exemplified in the vows of chastity and poverty. By the vow of chastity, the religious makes a special promise to abstain from all acts which are contrary to the virtue of holy purity, and, at the same time, vows to lead a life of celibacy. The difference

---

[1] Humphrey, *Elements of Religious Life*, p. 27–28.

[2] "Votum est sollemne, si ab Ecclesia uti tale fuerit agnitum; secus simplex." —Can. 1308 §2.

[3] "...consistit in vi...ipsis addita, irritos vel saltem irritabiles faciendi certos actus...votorum perfectioni contrarios."—Bouix, *De Jure Regularium*, pars. I, sec. III, cap 5.

between the simple and the solemn vow of chastity rests in the fact that the former is an impedient impediment for marriage, while the latter is a diriment impediment. A marriage contract, entered into by a religious in simple vows is valid, but gravely sinful—a sacrilige.[1] On the other hand, a marriage contract, entered into by a solemnly professed religious, besides being sacrilegious, is at the same time, absolutely null and void.[2] Against religious who violate their vow of chastity by marriage, or attempted marriage, the Church proceeds with grave penalties. The religious in simple vows who, without a dispensation, enters into a marriage contract, is by that very fact, excommunicated. Absolution from the censure is reserved to the Ordinary.[3] The solemnly professed religious who attempts marriage, even though it be by means of a civil contract, is likewise excommunicated. The censure in this case is reserved to the Holy See *simpliciter*.[4] Besides the penalty of excommunication, the religious, whether simply or solemnly professed, who thus violates his vow of chastity becomes irregular *ex delicto*.[5] Moreover, by the very fact of his committing this crime, the religious is dismissed from the religious state.[6] In order to make this dismissal effective, it is sufficient that the superior, in accordance with the prescriptions of his order or congregation, make a formal declaration of the fact.[7]

The vow of poverty may be described as the vow whereby the religious "promises God the renunciation of exterior property or riches which the legislation of his institute prescribes as the matter of the vow.[8] By the simple vow of poverty, the religious does not give up the ownership or *dominium* of his property. Whatever possessions the religious owned before, remain his own, even after he pronounces his simple vows. Nor does he, by the simple vow of poverty, relinquish the right to acquire other private property.[9] Any property which may come to the simply professed religious in the form of inheritance, legacy,

---

[1] "Nullum votum simplex irritat matrimonium, nisi irritatio speciali Sedis Apostolicæ præscripto pro aliquibus statuta fuerit."—Can. 1058 §2.

[2] "Item invalide matrimonium attentant religiosi qui vota sollemnia professi sunt..."—Can. 1073.

[3] Can. 2388 §2.

[4] Can. 2388 §1.

[5] Can. 985, 3°.

[6] Can. 646 §1, 3°.

[7] Can. 646 §2.

[8] Turner, *The Vow of Poverty*, p. xxxiii.

[9] Can. 580 §1.

donation, or through the settlement of outstanding debts, will be added to the sum total of the property he owned before his entrance into religion.[1] But what the same religious acquires by personal industry, or what is given to him, as a member of his institute, belongs not to the religious, but to the institute of which he is a member.[2] Although the simply professed religious retains ownership of his property as well as the right to acquire other property, he renounces the free and independent exercise of administration over the same. In virtue of his simple vow of poverty, the religious is forbidden to perform any act of administration without first obtaining the permission of his religious superior.[3] To act otherwise would be a violation of the vow. The act would be illicit, but nevertheless valid.[4]

By the solemn vow of poverty, on the other hand, the religious renounces not only the free and independent use and administration of his property, but he also gives up the very right of ownership. The solemnly professed religious is incapacitated both to own and to acquire temporalities. Whatever property or temporal goods the solemnly professed religious may acquire, he acquires not for himself, but for his order, if this order is capable of possessing, otherwise such acquisitions are acquired in the name of the Holy See.[5] The religious, in virtue of his solemn vow of poverty, is incapable also of performing any act of administration over temporalities without the permission of his proper superior. Any such act on the part of a solemnly professed religious, besides being illicit, as in the case of the religious in simple vows, is, at the same time, also invalid.[6]

---

[1] Turner, *The Vow of Poverty*, p. 144.

[2] "Quidquid autem industria sua vel intuitu religionis acquirit, religioni acquirit."—Can. 580 §2.

[3] Papi, *Religious in Church Law*, p. 236; Turner, *The Vow of Poverty*, p. 123.

[4] "Simplex professio, temporaria sit vel perpetua, actus votis contrarios reddit illicitos, sed non invalidos..."—Can. 579.

[5] "Post sollemnem professionem, salvis peculiaribus Apostolicæ Sedis indultis, omnia bona quæ quovis modo obveniunt regulari:

1. In Ordine capaci possidendi, cedunt Ordini vel provinciæ vel domui sesundum constitutiones;

2. In Ordini incapaci, acquiruntur Sanctæ Sedi in proprietatem."—Can. 582.

[6] "...actus votis contrarios reddit...professio autem sollemnis, si sint irritabiles, etiam invalidos."—Can. 579.

CHAPTER VIII

DISPOSITION OF PROPERTY BEFORE PROFESSION

The simple vow of poverty renders the religious incapable of the administration of temporal effects after his profession. But since such temporal effects are constantly in need of prudent administration, the Code makes various provisions in this matter. For the simply professed religious, it demands the appointment of an administrator, and the disposition of all revenues. Because the solemnly professed religious is incapable, not only of administrating, but also of possessing property, the Code demands that before his solemn profession he make a complete renunciation of any temporal effects he may possess.

ARTICLE 1.

APPOINTMENT OF ADMINISTRATOR AND DISPOSAL OF REVENUES

From the foregoing chapter it was seen that the simply professed religious, by his vow of poverty, deprives himself of the free and independent use and administration of his temporal possessions, without, however, renouncing the ownership over them. In order properly to provide for his property during the time of his simple profession, the Code demands that every novice, before making his simple profession, appoint a person of his own choice to carry on the administration in his stead, and at the same time to dispose freely, unless the constitutions prescribe otherwise, of both the use and usufruct of his property.[1]

[1] "Ante professionem votorum simplicium, sive temporariorum sive perpetuorum, novitius debet, ad totum tempus quo simplicibus votis adstringetur, bonorum suorum administrationem cedere cui maluerit et, nisi constitutiones aliud ferant, de eorundem usu et usufructu libere disponere."—Can. 569 §1.

The precept of this canon is binding on all novices, since in accordance with canon 574, all novices must make simple profession at the close of the novitiate year. No exact time is specified by the canon when its precept must be fulfilled; the canon states simply, *ante professionem.* The canon, however, seems to suggest that it should take place during the last weeks before the profession is to be made,[1] preferably after the council or chapter has decided in favor of the novice's being admitted to profession.[2] There is one phrase in the canon which is rather difficult to interpret. The canon demands that this disposition of the administration be made by the novice before simple vows SIVE TEMPORARIORUM SIVE PERPETUORUM. In canon 574, as already noted, the Code prescribes that all novices must make temporal profession for at least three years before they may be validly admitted to perpetual profession. The difficulty in the present canon is to reconcile the use of the words NOVICE and PERPETUAL PROFESSION. Authors have advanced various explanations to solve the difficulty. Blat[3] holds that the novice must make the appointment of an adminstrator as well as the disposition of the use of his property before he is admitted to temporal profession; but these acts, he further states, must be repeated, either implicitly, or explicitly, before the perpetual profession. They are implicitly repeated before the perpetual profession if no change is made in the former disposition; they are explicitly repeated when, with the proper permission of the religious superior, a change is made. This opinion lacks solid foundation.[4] Pruemmer[5] gives the following interpretation. The novice must make the necessary disposition before he is admitted to temporary profession. This is the ordinary method of procedure. But when a religious in accordance with the prescriptions of canon 634, transfers from one religious order or congregation to another, he must comply with the prescriptions of canon 569 §1, immediately before he is admitted to perpetual

---

[1] Schaefer, *De Religiosis*, p. 313, fn. 8.

[2] Bakalarczyk, *De Noviatu*, p. 187.

[3] *Commentarium*, II, 550.

[4] Pruemmer, *Manuale J. C.*, q. 212, fn. 85; Chelodi, *Jus de Personis*, p. 449, fn. 3; Larraona, *CpR*, I (1920), 336; Bakalarczyk, *De Noviatu*, p. 188; Turner, *The Vow of Poverty*, p. 122.

[5] *Manuale J. C.*, q. 212, c.

profession in the second congregation at the close of the novitiate made in this latter congregation.

Larraona[1] is of the opinion that the words *sive perpetuorum* have crept into the present edition of the Code because of an oversight. In the preparatory editions, which appeared at various intervals before the present edition was finally promulgated, it was not demanded that all religious, without exception, make temporal profession before being admitted to perpetual vows. In that case the application of the present canon would have had no difficulty, since then the disposition of adminstration before temporal profession would have been obligatory for those novices who would make temporary vows at the end of the year of probation, while novices of orders who would make perpetual profession immediately after their novitiate, would be obliged to comply with these demands of the present canon before their perpetual profession. But, Larraona continues, even now the clause *sive temporariorum sive perpetuorum* may have its practical application, in so far as the first part of the clause—*sive temporariorum*—has reference to all those novices who, according to the prescriptions of canon 574, make temporal profession immediately after the novitiate; the latter part of the clause—*sive perpetuorum*—may possibly refer to the religious who, by special privilege from the Holy See, are exempt from the prescriptions of canon 574, and make perpetual profession at the end of the year of probation. Such a privilege has been granted to the Jesuits, and to the Sisters of the Sacred Heart.[2] Although the opinions of both Pruemmer and Larraona have intrinsic probability, the opinion of Larraona seems to be the more favored among authors.[3]

The appointment of the administrator, and the disposal of the use and usufruct is to be made, not for a definite period of time, but for the entire duration of the simple profession. It is to remain in force for the entire time which the novice will spend in simple profession, be it temporal or perpetual. It, however,

---

[1] *CpR*, I (1920), 335.

[2] *Periodica*, X (1922), p. (13).

[3] Goyeneche, *CpR*, II (1921), 145; Bakalarczyk, *De Novitiatu*, p. 188; Turner, *The Vow of Poverty*, p. 121.

automatically ceases just as soon as the religious leaves the religious state,[1] or when he makes solemn profession.

The novice is entirely free to choose as his adminstrator whomsoever he desires. The administrator may be a relative, or a friend of the novice; or, if he so desires, he may appoint the institute of which he will become a member by profession. In making the appointment, the Code prescribes no formalities that need be followed. The novice may simply entrust his property to the care of the person whom he chooses, with the agreement that it be returned to him on demand.[2] It would be more safe, however, to have all the details of the appointment drafted in the form of a legal document.

The administration of all the property which the novice actually possesses at the time of his profession must be included in the appointment.[3] There is no obligation of extending this administration to include such property to which the novice has either a right to obtain, or that which he has only a well-founded hope of receiving. This seems to be the mind of the legislator, since in §2 of the same canon, he makes provisions for property which may come into the possession of the religious after he has made his profession. But, on the other hand, there is nothing to forbid the novice's including such possible future acquisitions should he choose to do so.[4]

Besides appointing an administrator for his property, the novice is further obliged to dispose of the use and usufruct of the same property. By USE is understood the right to enjoy the property, while by USUFRUCT is meant the enjoyment of, not only the property, but also the fruits and profits derived from the property—in a word, usufruct is the enjoyment of all the revenues accruing from the property.[5]

In making the disposal of his revenues, the novice is entirely free in his choice of both the person who is to receive the reve-

---

[1] "...per discessum autem a religione eiusmodi cessio ac dispositio habere vim desinit."—Can. 580, §3.

[2] Turner, *The Vow of Poverty*, p. 124.

[3] Larraona, *CpR*, I (1920), 338; Turner, *The Vow of Poverty*, p. 120; Bakalarczyk, *De Novitiatu*, p. 189.

[4] Turner, *The Vow of Poverty*, p. 121.

[5] Noldin, *De Præceptis*, nn. 360–361; Sabetti-Barrett, *Compendium Theologiæ Moralis*, p. 366; Papi, *Religious in Church Law*, p. 254.

nues, and of the manner and conditions of the disposal. The only limitation made by the legislator is expressed in the words of the canon: '*nisi constitutiones aliud ferant.*' In reference to this limitation, the Pontifical Commission for the Interpretation of the Code, in a response issued on October 16, 1919, stated that in this point, constitutions approved before the promulgation of the Code, must be obeyed, even though they either limit, or altogether deprive, the novice of his right to dispose freely the revenues accruing from his property.[1] This limitation will likewise be effective in case constitutions approved after the Code make similar restrictions.[2]

A novice who did not comply with the prescriptions of canon 569 §1, because before his profession he was not the owner of any property, is obliged to appoint an administrator and dispose of his revenues, if after his profession any property comes into his possession. So, likewise, a simply professed religious, who acquires new possessions after his profession, must make provisions for the proper administration of the newly acquired property.[3] In case the religious, later on, desires to make any change, either in the administration of his property, or in the disposal of the revenues accruing therefrom, he may not, unless the constitutions of his institution grant a general permission, do so without the permission of the proper religious superior.[4]

Article 2.

THE LAST WILL OF SIMPLY PROFESSED RELIGIOUS

In order to forestall the possibility of any troublesome litigation in the disposal of the property of simply professed religious after death, the Code, very wisely demands that, before making temporal profession, every novice for congregations must,

---

[1] *AAS*, XI (1919), 478.

[2] Turner, *The Vow of Poverty*, p. 129.

[3] "Ea cessio ac dispositio, si prætermissa fuerit ob defectum bonorum et hæc postea supervenerit, aut si facta fuerit et postea alia bona quovis titulo obvenerint, fiat aut iteretur secundum normas §1 statutas, non obstante simplici professione emissa."—Can. 569 §2.

[4] Can. 580 §3.

by will, arrange for the disposal of his property after his death.[1] The prescription of making a will is obligatory on all novices who enter religious institutes which make only simple vows. Though not expressly included, the obligation seems to extend also to those religious who, because of local circumstances, make only simple vows by special indult of the Holy See.[2] Novices who will make solemn profession after their term of temporal profession do not come under the prescriptions of this law. They are not, however, forbidden to make a will for the time that they will spend in simple profession before being admitted to solemn vows. In fact, such a procedure would prove very beneficial, should the novice be called by death before being admitted to make his solemn profession.[3] In defining the subjects of the prescription, the Code uses the term *novitius*. Since the canon has no retroactive force,[4] all religious who made profession in congregations before the Code finally went into effect on May 19, 1918, are not now bound to comply with this obligation. But a failure on the part of novices to comply with the obligation since the Code went into effect, affords no ground for exemption; these must satisfy the dictates of the canon, even after their profession has taken place.[5]

The obligation to make the will is present even though at the time of his temporal profession, the novice possesses no property or other temporal effects. The canon in question expressly states that the will is to provide for, not only property which the novice actually owns at the time of his profession, but also any property that may in the course of time be acquired by him in any way whatsoever.[6] Just as in the appointment of his administrator and in the disposal of his revenues, so also in the making of his will, the novice is absolutely free in the choice of his beneficiaries.

---

[1] Novitius in Congregatione religiosa ante professionem votorum temporariorum testamentum de bonis præsentibus vel forte obventuris libere condat. —Can. 569 §3.

[2] Turner, *The Vow of Poverty*, p. 165.

[3] Cf. Schaefer, *De Religiosis*, p. 319; Fanfani, *De Jure Religiosorum*, p. 228; Bakalarczyk, *De Novitiatu*, p. 190; Turner, *The Vow of Poverty*, p. 165.

[4] Can. 10.

[5] Schaefer, *De Religiosis*, p. 318; Fanfani, *De Jure Religiosorum*, p. 228; Turner, *The Vow of Poverty*, p. 166; Papi, *Religious in Church Law*, p. 258.

[6] Bakalarczyk, *De Novitiatu*, p. 191; *CpR*, IV (1923), 282.

A controversy has arisen as to the existence of an obligation to make the required will before the profession if, at the time, the novice is not of the necessary age to make a will which the civil law will recognize as valid and enforceable. Some authors[1] hold that under such circumstances, the novice is not obliged to make the will until he can do so validly in the eyes of the civil law. Larraona, moreover, is of the opinion that if the will is not valid in civil law, it will also be canonically invalid.[2] Other authorities[3] assert that circumstances which would militate against a civilly valid will do not free the novice from complying with the dictates of the present canon. The novice must satisfy the demands of canon 569 §2, before his temporary profession, then in due time ratify the will in the eyes of the civil law, if necessary. This opinion seems to be the more probable, since the present canon, in so far as it refers to novices, would be quite useless; most novices make their first profession before they have attained the age of majority. This opinion has received added weight by reason of an unpublished private response given to the Superior General of the Redemptorists, in which the Pontifical Commission for the Interpretation of the Code stated that novices are obliged to make their will in accordance with the dictates of canon 569 §3, before their temporal profession, even though this will would be civilly invalid; the Commission added, however, that a ratification before the civil law must be obtained as soon as circumstances permit.[4]

After his profession, the religious may not make any changes in the will, without first obtaining permission from the Holy See. But in case of an emergency, when time will not permit this recourse, the Code authorizes the major superior to grant the neces-

---

[1] Larraona, *CpR*, II (1921), 10; Goyeneche, *CpR*, V (1924), 439–440; Bakalarczyk, *De Novitiatu*, 192; Jansen, *Ordensrecht*, p. 117.

[2] "...nos credimus non solum non adesse obligationem testamentum redigendi si ipsum condi civiliter valide non potest, sed etiam per testamentum iure civili invalidum, quia ad formam iuris non factum, obligationem non adimpleri ab hoc can. 569 §3 impositam..."*CpR*, II (1921), 10, fn. 3.

[3] Vermeersch-Creusen, *Epitome*, I, 417–418; Fanfani, *De Jure Religiosorum*, p. 228; Schaefer, *De Religiosis*, p. 318; Pejska, *Jus Canonicum Religiosorum*, p. 100; Turner, *The Vow of Poverty*, p. 167; Gearing, "The Confessor and the Vow of Poverty," — *AER.*, 61 (1919), 143; Papi, *Religious in Church Law*, p. 252; Woywod, *Practical Commentary*, I, 242.

[4] Cf. Turner, *The Vow of Poverty*, p. 167, fn. 178.

sary permission; in case that the urgency of the cause is such that recourse to the major superior is likewise impossible, then the religious may act with the permission of his immediate local superior.[1]

ARTICLE 3

RENUNCIATION OF PROPERTY BEFORE SOLEMN PROFESSION

The solemn vow of poverty renders the solemnly professed religious incapable of either acquiring or owning any temporal effects in his own name. Before making his solemn profession, the candidate must make a complete renunciation of any property he may happen to possess. In order to protect novices from making a premature renutiation, the Council of Trent declared that no novice could validly renounce any property, except within two months of the day set for his solemn profession. Any renunciation made contrary to the decree of the Council, even though it had been confirmed by oath, would be invalid. Furthermore, in order to make the renunciation within the two month period before the profession, the permission of the bishop or of his vicar, was required.[2] The Council expressly exempted from this decree the novices of the Society of Jesus.[3]

The substance of this Tridentine regulation has been retained in the present legislation of the Code. The Code, in canon 581 §1, declares that no simply professed religious may validly dispose by renunciation, of any property or temporal effects, except within sixty days before the date of his solemn profession.

[1] "Professus a votis simplicibus in Congregationibus religiosis non licet testamentum conditum ad normam can. 569 §3, mutare sine licentia Sanctæ Sedis, vel si res urgeat nec tempus suppetat ad eam recurrendi, sine licentia Superioris maioris aut, si nec ille adiri possit, localis."—Can. 583, 2°.

[2] "Nulla quoque renunciatio, antea facta etiam cum juramento, vel in favorem cujuscumque causæ piæ, valeat, nisi cum licentia episcopi sive ejus vicarii fiat, intra duos menses proximos ante professionem; ac non alias intelligatur effectum suum sortiri, nisi secuta professione: aliter vero facta, etiamsi cum hujus favoris expressa renunciatione, etiam jurata, sit irrita, et nullius effectus..." Sess. XXV, *De regul. et monial.*, cap. 16.

[3] "Per hæc tamen sancta Synodus non intendit aliquid innovare, aut prohibere, quin religio clericorum societatis Jesu, juxta pium eorum institutum, a sancta Sede apostolica approbatum, Domino, et ejus Ecclesiæ inservire possint;..." *ibid.*

Within those sixty days, however, which immediately precede the solemn profession, the religious is obliged to renounce, in favor of whomsoever he desires, all the property and other temporal goods he possesses, or over which he exercises the right of ownership. In making this renunciation, however, he must affix as a condition for its effectiveness, that he actually make valid, solemn vows.[1] From this general law the Code exempts those religious institutes who have received any special indults from the Holy See, concerning any one of the points expressed in the canon. In virtue of such a special indult some religious in Belgium and Holland may not only retain ownership of property after solemn profession, but they may also acquire new property.[2]

The renunciation of property which the Code in canon 581 §1, demands of every candidate for solemn profession, is an actual "abdication of ownership;" it consists in giving up all temporal possessions and depriving oneself of the right, not only to own, but also to acquire and to administer, temporalities.[3]

The renunciation should take place in the form of an absolute donation *inter vivos*.[4] A will, or a donatio *mortis causa* does not satisfy the demands of the canon,[5] because by a will the testator does not give up the right of ownership, since neither the will, nor the donation *mortis causa* becomes effective until after the death of the testator; moreover, either can be revoked or altered at any thime during the lifetime of the testator. Solemn profession, however, incapacitates the religious both to own property and to exercise adminstration. Hence this renunciation demanded by the present canon, must so be made that the religious gives up all rights and claims on the property he renounces.

The demands of the canon must be complied with within sixty days, immediately preceding the date of the solemn pro-

---

[1] "Professus a votis simplicibus antea nequit valide, sed intra sexaginta dies ante professionem sollemnem, salvis peculiaribus indultis a Sancte Sede concessis, debet omnibus bonis quæ actu habet, cui maluerit, sub conditione secuturæ professionis, renuntiare."—Can. 581 §1.

[2] Vermeersch-Creusen, *Epitome*, I, 436.

[3] Augustine, *Commentary*, III, 282; Papi, *Religious Profession*, p. 67.

[4] Turner, *The Vow of Poverty*, p. 184.

[5] Augustine, *Commentary*, III, 282; Papi, *Religious Profession*, p. 67; Turner, *The Vow of Poverty*, p. 184.

fession. These sixty days must be computed in accordance with the norms of canon 34 §3, 3°, so that a religious whose solemn profession will take place on July 11, must make the renunciation some time between the midnight beginning May 12, and the time of the profession. But if the day of the solemn profession is postponed for any reason, the renunciation of property made within the sixty days preceding the day on which the profession should have taken place, will not be invalidated on that account.[1]

The renunciation must always be made with the condition that it becomes effective only if, and when the solemn profession takes place. It does not, however, seem necessary that this condition be expressed in the renunciation, because it is contained in the canon which treats of the renunciation, in the words: "*sub conditione secuturæ professionis.*" Therefore, by the very fact that the profession does not take place, the renunciation becomes null and void.

In choosing the beneficiary, the religious is free to select whomsoever he desires. He may divide his possessions among his relatives and friends; he may choose to devote them to some pious cause, or he may bestow them upon the community of which he is a member. The religious needs no permission to make the renunciation. According to the regulations of the Council of Trent, cited above, the renunciation could not be made validly without first obtaing the permission of the bishop or of his vicar. By remaining silent on this point, the Code abrogates this particular point of the former legislation, in consequence of which, the renunciation may be made both licitly and validly without the permission of either the bishop, of his vicar, or of the religious superior.[2]

The renunciation must include all property which the religious actually owns at the time of his solemn profession. Authors propose this question: Can the religious, in his renunciation, include also property which will come to him after his solemn profession? Such future property may be divided into two classes: 1. property to which he has a right, such as inheritances, in

---

[1] Schmalzgrueber, *Jus Ecclesiasticum Universum*, lib. III, pars. IV, tit. XXXI, n. 106, sq.; Piat, *Prælectiones Juris Regularis*, I, 129; Augustine, *Commentary*, III, 282; Turner, *The Vow of Poverty*, p. 183.

[2] Schaefer, *De Religiosis*, p. 349; Papi, *Religious Profession*, p. 68; Turner, *The Vow of Poverty*, p. 183.

countries where children are necessary heirs; 2. property which the religious has only a hope of receiving, such as legacies which relatives may possibly will to him. The common opinion among authors holds that property to which the religious has a right may be included in the renunciation.[1] Concerning the second class of property—that which the religious has a hope of receiving, a distinction must be made. If the hope which the religious entertains has a solid foundation, he may include the property in his renunciation,[2] because, as Fanfani remarks, the well-founded hope which the religious has of obtaining this property is *pretio æstimabilis*. But property which the religious has no well-founded hope of obtaining, is not *pretio æstimabilis* and, therefore, he may not include it when he makes the required renunciation.[3]

This renunciation of property becomes obligatory in conscience the moment the religious pronounces his solemn profession. But in order to make it enforceable also in civil law, the Code demands that as soon as possible after the solemn profession has been made, all the requirements of civil law, in reference to the validity of renunciation before the civil courts, be minutely complied with.[4]

---

[1] This opinion is held by such authorities as Larraona, *CpR*, I (1920), 79, 183; Vermeersch-Creusen, *Epitome*, I, 436; Papi, *Religious in Church Law*, 259–260; Turner, *The Vow of Poverty*, p. 186. The opinion has a firm foundation in a response of the Congregation of Bishops and Regulars given under date of Sept. 16, 1885—*Fontes*, 2011.

[2] Larraona, *CpR*, I (1920), 78, 183; Blat, *Commentarium*, II, 644; Fanfani, *De Jure Religiosorum*, p. 298; Turner, *The Vow of Poverty*, p. 186; *et al.*

[3] Larraona, *CpR*, I (1920), 79–80, 182; Fanfani, *De Jure Religiosorum*, p. 297–298; Blat, *Commentarium*, II, 644; Turner, *The Vow of Poverty*, p. 186.

[4] "Secuta professione, ea omnia statim fiant, quæ sunt necessaria ut renuntiatio etiam iure civili effectum consequatur."—Can. 581 §2.

CHAPTER IX

CEREMONIAL AND RECORDING OF PROFESSION

Canon 576

§1. In emittenda professione religiosa servetur præscriptus in constitutionibus ritus.

§2. Documentum emissæ professionis, ab ipso professo et saltem ab eo coram quo professio emissa est, subscriptum, servetur in tabulario religionis; et insuper, si agatur de professione sollemni, Superior eam excipiens debet profitentis parochum baptismi de eadem certiorem reddere, ad normam can. 470 §2.

ARTICLE 1

THE CEREMONIAL

The ceremonial of religious profession embraces all the rites and ceremonies with which the act of profession is clothed, in order to add to its dignity and external solemnity. It includes, in general, the reading of the profession formula, the prayers, the blessing of the religious habit, and the like, which accompany the making of vows. The Code, in the first paragraph of canon 576, establishes no definite regulations concerning this ceremonial, but directs simply that the prescriptions of the constitutions of each order and congregation on this point, be observed. It is well to note here that, unless the individual constitutions rule otherwise, the non-observance of any point of the prescribed ceremonial will not affect the validity of the profession, because these rites and ceremonies are merely accidentals added to the act of profession.[1]

[1] Augustine, *Commentary*, III, 263.

The Holy See has, in the past, issued several instructions concerning the ceremonies of profession of religious women, which may not be overlooked. When, in virtue of the decree "*Perpensis*," simple perpetual vows were established for orders of women as a preparation for solemn profession, doubts arose concerning an appropriate ceremonial to be carried out. On July 28, 1902, the Sacred Congregation of Bishops and Regulars declared that the customary ritual formula, formerly followed for the making of solemn profession, should now be used for the simple perpetual profession, with this change, that any word or phrase, expressive of solemn profession, should be avoided. Solemn profession, the instruction continued, need be nothing more than a renewal of vows, made privately, without ceremony, into the hands of the proper superioress, before the assembled community.[1] Again, on January 15, 1903, in response to a question proposed by Cardinal de Skrbensky, the Archbishop of Prague, the same Congregation stated that if the superioress and the community so desired, the solemn profession could take place publicly before the bishop or his delegate, but that in any case, nothing more was necessary than that the simply professed religious read the formula of profession, expressing that the vows are solemn.[2]

It is quite evident why the Congregation desired that the complete ceremonial, inclusive of the blessing and bestowal of the veil and ring, should take place at the profession of the simple vows. These preparatory simple vows, as prescribed by the decree "*Perpensis*," were perpetual on the part of the religious making them; hence it was only logical that in the ceremonies the symbolism expressing this perpetuity should be carried out for the simple profession, since the subsequent solemn profession was only a renewal and confirmation of the former.[3]

New difficulties arose when, with the promulgation of the Code, it became obligatory that perpetual profession, both simple and solemn, be preceded by preparatory temporary vows. Hence the Sacred Congregation of Religious, on the 10th of July, 1919, reversed the former decisions of the Congregation of Bishops and

---

1 S. C. Ep. et Reg., *Bononiensis*, 28 Jul. 1902—*Fontes*, n. 2040.

2 *Fontes*, n. 2043.

3 Maroto, *CpR*, I (1920), 292.

Regulars, by stating that all ceremonies, symbolic of perpetuity, should be reserved for the solemn profession.

An resolutiones S. C. EE et RR., sub die 18 Julii, 1902 ad I, et 15 Januarii 1903 ad I et II, circa modum servandum in emittenda simplici et sollemni Monialium professione post editum decretum "Perpensis" diei 3 Maii 1902 vigeant post inductam a Codice Juris Canonici professionem votorum temporaneorum, quæ votis sollemnibus præmitti debeat?

S. Congregatio, omnibus mature perpensis, respondendum censuit: Negative, et ad mentem. Mens est ut professioni sollemni reserventur ritus illi omnes et cæremoniæ quæ ad perpetuitatem status referuntur; ad professionem vero temporaneam sufficit ut ad normam canonis 572 §1, 6°, a legitimo Superiore secundum Constitutiones per se vel per alium recipiatur.—*AAS*, XI (1919) 323.

Although this instruction has direct reference only to profession in orders of women with solemn vows, it may, with proper limitations, be applied also to professions of simple vow congregations.[1] Just what ceremonies and symbols are to be considered as strictly expressive of perpetuity is difficult to establish. According to Fanfani[2] and Kinane,[3] the blessing and bestowal of the veil and ring should be reserved to the perpetual profession, while on the other hand, De Meester considers that these ceremonies do not necessarily imply perpetuity, and that in consequence they need not be excluded from the ceremonial of the temporal profession.[4] In view of the difference of opinion on the subject, either opinion may safely be followed. Hence any ceremonial prescribing the blessing and bestowal of the ring or veil for the temporal profession need not be changed, unless the Congregation of Religious should later on declare that such ceremonies are expressive of absolute perpetuity.

The act of profession may take place before the Blessed Sacrament, exposed. This was expressly declared by the Sacred Congregation of Rites, on May 18, 1878.[5] Profession may like-

---

[1] Cf. Maroto, *CpR*, I (1920), 295.

[2] *De Jure Religiosorum*, p. 286.

[3] *IER*, XXIX (1927), 637.

[4] *J. C. Compendium*, II, n. 1006.

[5] Cf. *Ephemerides Liturgicæ*, VII (1893), 100; *NRT*, XXVI (1894), 578.

wise be made during the Holy Sacrifice of the Mass. In a general decree, issued by the same Congregation, on August 14, 1894,[1] the following method for making profession during the Holy Sacrifice is described: After the *Confiteor*, the *Misereatur*, *Indulgentiam*, and *Ecce Agnus Dei* have been recited, the celebrant will turn toward the candidates and hold up before them the Sacred Host. Each candidate will then recite the formula of profession, and immediately receive the Sacred Host.[2] This same ceremony, but with a slight alteration, is also to be used when the renewal of profession is to take place duting rhe Holy Sacrifice. In the ceremonial of the renewal, the celebrant remains turned toward the altar until after the religious have recited the formula of renewal in common, after which he will bring Holy Communion to each.[3]

The method of making profession during the Sacrifice of the Mass, as described by this decree of the Congregation of Rites, is to be followed by all religious congregations, both male and female, whose constitutions prescribe that the profession is to take place during Mass, while the celebrant is holding the Sacred Host. This was declared by the same Congregation on June 5, 1896.[4] Since the decree of August 27, 1894, was issued for religious congregations, it is not binding for religious orders, even though their constitutions prescribe that profession is to be made during the Sacrifice of the Mass. Moreover, if the constitutions

---

[1] *Decreta Authentica*, S. C. Rit., n. 3836.

[2] "...Celebrans profitentium vota excepturus, sumpto Sanctissimo Eucharistiæ Sacramento, absoluta Confessione ac verbis quæ ante fidelium Communionem dici solent, Sacram Nostiam manu tenens, ad profitentes sese convertet: hi vero singuli, alta voce, professionem legent, ac postquam quisque legerit, statim Sanctissimum Eucharistiæ Sacramentum sumet..."—S. C. Rit., *Decr. Authen.* n. 3836.

[3] "...In renovatione autem votorum, Celebrans ad altare conversus expectet donec renovantes votorum formulam protulerint; qui, nisi pauci sint, omnes simul, uno præeunte formulam renovationis recitabunt, ac postea ex ordine Sacratissimum Corpus Domini accipient..."—*Ibid.*

[4] "A Sacra Congregatione Ritum expostulatum fuit: An decretum Generale ab eadem S. Rituum Congregatione die 27 Augusti 1894 editum, quo, ad omnem ambiguitatem tollendam et uniformitatem inducendam, methodus in professione et renovatione votorum intra Missam servanda statuitur, vi obligandi polleat penes quaslibet religiosas utriusque sexus Congregationes?

Et Sacra Rituum Congregatio, ad relationem infrascripti Secretarii, omni-

of a congregation prescribe that the profession is to take place during another part of the Mass, after the Gospel, for instance, it is not necessary that the constitutions be altered to conform to this method of making profession, because, as appears from the response of June 5, 1896, this method is to be followed only when profession takes place after the consecration of the Mass.[1] The *raison d'être* of the decree of the Congregation is not so much to prescribe a method of making profession, as it is to guard against any abuses which might creep in. It must here be added that the Congregation of Rites, in the general decree of August 27, 1894, cited above, expressly prohibited embodying in the Constitutions, the method of making profession during Mass, described in the decree.

Article 2

RECORDING

In the second paragraph of canon 576, the Code prescribes that an authentic record be kept of every profession. The fundamental idea of this prescription dates back to the Rule of St. Benedict. In the fifty-eighth chapter, on the receiving of candidates, he prescribed that when a novice is to be admitted to his profession, he must draw up his profession in writing; this document is then placed on the altar and later removed by the abbot and preserved in the monastery, to be used against the neo-professed, should he later on abandon his vocation. In the course of time other methods of recording profession were devised. As early as the ninth century there existed in the monastery of St. Gall a special book into which the novices inscribed their

bus mature perpensis, proposito Dubio respondendum censuit: AFFIRMATIVE, UBI VOTA NUNCUPANTUR VEL RENOVANTUR INTRA MISSAM CORAM CELEBRANTE SACRAM HOSTIAM MANU TENENTE.

Atque ita rescripsit. Die 5 Junii, 1896.

Cai. Card. Aloisi-Masella, S.C.R., Præfect.

Aloisius Tripepi, Secretarius. "—*Ephemerides Liturgicæ*, X (1896), 450; *ASS*, XXVIII (1895–1896), 798. This response is likewise contained in the *Decreta Authentica S. C. Rit.* as number 3912, but here the words: "Coram celebrante Sacram Hostiam Manu tenente" have been omitted.

[1] Jansen, *Ordensrecht*, p. 127.

professions.[1] Clement VIII, in his constitution "*Cum ad Regularem*," of March 19, 1603, prescribed that a book of this kind be kept in every monastery.[2]

The Code leaves optional the method of keeping this record, prescribing simply that a document, signed by the neo-professed and at least the superior into whose hands the profession was made, be kept in the monastery archives, as a public record of the act. In complying with this prescription, various methods may be employed. A special book or register may be provided, into which each neo-professed inscribes his name, together with the proper information as to the nature and duration of the profession, and the date on which the profession was made. Each set of entries must then be signed by the proper superior. Again, a single document, containing the necessary data may be drawn up for each profession-class, which is then signed by each member of the class and the superior. Finally, each individual profession formula, containing the necessary information, and bearing the signature of the professed and that of the superior, may be filed.[3] No matter what method is followed, each record must have at least two signatures, that of the neo-professed, and that of the person into whose hands the profession was made. In cases, such as occur particularly in the profession of religious women, when the profession is received by a delegated person, it may be well that, to the signature of the delegate, the religious superior add also his own signature. The document may likewise be signed by other witnesses, if the constitutions so demand.[4] This record constitutes a public document, and as such will be admitted as testimony in any court of justice should the occasion present itself.[5]

Canon 576 §2, finally prescribes that when the profession was solemn, the superior must transmit a notification of the fact to the parish in which the neo-professed had received baptism, so that it may be recorded in the baptismal register as required

---

[1] Herwegen, *Geschichte der Benediktinischen Professformel*, p. 33 sq.

[2] *Bull. Rom.*, X, 776.

[3] Jansen, *Ordensrecht*, p. 127; Brandys, *Kirchliches Rechtsbuch*, p. 46.

[4] Vermeersch-Creusen, *Epitome*, I, 429; Fanfani, *De Jure Religiosorum*, p. 287; Brandys, *Kirchliches Rechtsbuch*, p. 46.

[5] Canons 1812, 1813 §1, 4°.

by canon 470 §2.[1] The reason for this is evident. Solemn profession constitutes a diriment matrimonial impediment.[2] Any information of this kind should be found in the baptismal register.

The canon requires the transmission of this information only for solemn profession. But according to canon 1073, through a special disposition of the Holy See, simple profession may likewise be made a diriment impediment for contracting marriage. This has been done in the case of the simple vows made by Jesuit Scholastics.[3] It would seem, therefore, that also in such cases, this notification should find its way into the baptismal register.[4]

The notification in question must be sent to the parish in which the professed was baptized. But when the parish of baptism is situated in Russia, this notification is not sent to the proper pastor, but to the special Commission for Russia in Rome.[5]

---

[1] "In libro baptizatorum adnotetur quoque si baptizatus...professionem sollemnem emiserit, eæque adnotationes in documenta accepti baptismatis semper referantur."—C. 470 §2.

[2] Canons 579, 1073.

[3] Const. "*Ascendente Domino,*" §22—*Fontes*, n. 153.

[4] "Si certa de re desit expressum præscriptum legis sive generalis sive particularis norma sumenda est...a legibus latis in similibus..."—Can. 20.

[5] Comm. Russ., 13 Jul. 1928—*AAS*, XX (1928), 260.

CHAPTER X

CONVALIDATION AND SANATION OF INVALID PROFESSION

Canon 586

§1. Professio religiosa irrita ob impedimentum externum non convalescit per subsequentes actus, sed opus est ut a Sede Apostolica sanetur, vel denuo, cognita nullitate et impedimento sublato, legitime emmittatur.

§2. Si autem irrita fuerit ob consensus defectum mere internum, hoc præstito, convalescit, dummodo ex parte religionis consensus non fuerit revocatus.

§3. Si contra validitatem professionis religiosæ gravia sint argumenta et religiosus renuat ad cautelam sive professionem renovare sive eiusdem sanationem petere, res ad Sedem Apostolicam deferatur.

In the foregoing chapters the requirements of Canon Law for the validity and liceity of religious profession have been proposed. A non-observance of any one of the points which the Code requires as a condition for validity will render the profession null and void, without any juridical obligatory force on either the religious or the community. Only by applying the proper remedies can such a situation be corrected. Neither prescription[1] nor the performance of any subsequent act, proper only to a professed religious, such as taking part in chapter proceedings, will validate an invalid profession.[2] The Code, in canon 586, provides two means of validating an invalid profession. These means are simple convalidation and the *sanatio in radice*.

---

[1] Pejska, *Jus Canonicum Religiosorum*, p. 114.

[2] "...non convalescit per subsequentes actus..."—Can. 586 §1; "Non firmatur tractu temporis, quod de jure ab initio non subsistit."—Reg. 18, R. J. in VI°.

Simple convalidation is the ordinary means of rectifying an invalid profession. It comprises a two-fold act: first, the removal of the obstacle, or impediment, and second, the renewal of the consent. The impediment causing the profession to be invalid may be an external one—one which is caused by the non-observance of any of the conditions prescribed for the validity of profession—such as a lack of the required age, a defective novitiate, a want of jurisdiction, or of proper delegation on the part of the person who receives the profession; the profession may also be invalid for a want of the internal consent. In either case, convalidation will have a different mode of procedure.

If an external impediment caused the profession to be invalid, this impediment must first be removed; this done, a new profession must be made.[1] In removing the invalidating cause, one of two ways may be adopted. The first, and ordinary way, is simply to supply the defect by completely satisfying the juridical requirement which had been neglected in making the profession. Thus, for instance, when an invalid novitiate was the cause of the invalid profession, the defect may be remedied by repeating the novitiate. The second way of removing the impediment is by a dispensation from the Holy See. This second method for removing the impediment should be resorted to when grave inconvenience or scandal would result from following the first method. Once the impediment has been removed, a new profession must be made. If the impediment which caused the invalid profession was publicly known, or if it is publicly known that the profession was invalidly made, then the new profession must be made publicly; but if the invalidity of the first profession is not known publicly, it will be sufficient to make the new profession in private before the legitimate superior, and in the presence of two witnesses, if the latter are required by the constitutions.[2] This procedure seems evident from an analogy between the convalidation of profession and that of an invalid marriage.[3]

When the invalidity of the profession was caused by the lack of internal consent, the profession is convalidated by simply

---

[1] Can. 586 §1.

[2] Pejska, *Jus Canonicum Religiosorum*, p. 114.

[3] Cf. can. 1136, §3.

supplying, internally, the defect, provided always that in the meantime the consent of the second party of the profession contract has not been revoked.[1] Hence, if a religious, when making his profession, went through the external formalities of profession without, however, giving his internal consent, he may at any time invalidate his profession by supplying the consent he had withheld. This may be done without any external formality taking place. But only then will such an invalid profession become valid and binding, if in the meantime the religious community has not withdrawn its consent.

The second method for rectifying an invalid profession is the *sanatio in radice.* From an analogy between the *sanatio* for religious profession mentioned in canon 586 §1, and that described in the canons referring to the sanation of invalid marriage, this *sanatio* may be defined as a mode of rectifying an invalid profession which, besides granting a dispensation from the impediment which caused the invalidity of profession, dispenses also from the obligation of renewing the profession, and by a fiction of law, has retroactive force in so far as it gives to the validated profession all the canonical effects which it would have had, if the profession had been valid from the very beginning.[2] The *sanatio* has a three-fold effect: 1. it dispenses from the impediment which caused the invalidity of the profession. Thus if the profession was invalid because of a defective novitiate, the *sanatio* frees the religious from the obligation of correcting the defect by a repetition of the year of probation. 2. It dispenses from the obligation of making a new profession. By the very fact that the *sanatio* is granted, the invalid profession becomes valid without any act on the part of the religious. 3. The *sanatio* extends the effects of the validated profession back to the moment when the invalid profession was made; but the invalid profession itself becomes valid only from the moment when the *sanatio* is granted. To illustrate: a religious makes profession, invalidly, on January 1, 1930, for which a *sanatio* is granted on January 1, 1931. The invalid profession becomes valid only from the moment when the *sanatio* is granted, in the present case, on January 1, 1931. But the effects of the validated profession are extended back to

[1] Can. 586 §2.

[2] Cf. can. 1138 §1.

the moment when the invalid profession was made. For example: seniority in a religious community is reckoned according to the day of profession; in the case cited above, let it be supposed that at various intervals between January 1, 1930, and January 1, 1931, five religious were validly professed in the community. The religious whose invalid profession was validated by means of the *sanatio*, on January 1, 1931, will be senior to all the religious who made profession after January 1, 1930. Or again: if by the constitutions, a religious receives the right of active and passive vote, after having been professed for ten years, this period must be reckoned from the time of his first profession.[1] In the case cited above, the ten-year period will be counted, not from January 1, 1931—the day on which the *sanatio* was granted, but from January 1, 1930—the day on which his first profession took place.

The *sanatio in radice* must be resorted to in extraordinary instances, when the ordinary means of convalidation would entail a serious inconvenience, when grave scandal would result, or when a large number of professions are in need of convalidation. An example of such an instance is the sanatio granted by the Holy See to a certain Congregation of Sisters of the Sacred Heart and Perpetual Adoration, whereby their professions were validated because during the period of the novitiate, they had not worn the religious habit.[2] The granting of the *sanatio* is reserved to the Congregation of Religious, to which Congregation all applications for the favor must be directed.

Under no conditions may a religious be permitted to continue to live in doubt as to the validity of his profession.[3] The doubt must be solved for either the validity or invalidity of the profession, and in the latter case the proper steps must be taken to rectify the profession. But if after diligent investigation, the doubt cannot be solved, then a *sanatio ad cautelam* must be applied for to the Holy See. If the religious whose profession is doubtful, refuses to take the proper steps to resolve the doubt, or to seek the precautionary convalidation, the entire case must be submitted to the Congregation of Religious for solution.[4]

---

[1] Can. 578, 3°.

[2] *ASS*, 41 (1908), 142.

[3] Fanfani, *De Jure Religiosorum*, p. 285; Schaefer, *De Religiosis*, p. 356.

[4] Can. 586 §3.

APPENDIX I

OBLIGATORY MILITARY SERVICE AND RELIGIOUS PROFESSION

On January 1, 1911, the Sacred Congregation of Religious issued the decree "*Inter Reliquas*,"[1] which contained a mode of procedure for the admission to religious profession of such young men who had not yet satisfied the law of their country with regard to the compulsory military training. This decree, as at first intended, was but a temporary measure, and as such was not incorporated in the Code. But because the trying circumstances which gave occasion for the issuance of the decree have not yet abated, a response to a *dubium*, presented to the same Congregation, declared that, with but a few alterations made necessary by new legislation contained in the Code, the decree, "*Inter Reliquas*," is still in force.[2] Hence in countries where the law of compulsory military service is in force, the prescriptions of the decree "*Inter Reliquas*," with some modifications, must be observed, not only for the liceity, but also for the validity, of religious profession.

According to the prescriptions of the above mentioned decree, "*Inter Reliquas*," no member of a religious order may be validly admitted to solemn profession, and no member of a simple vow congregation may be validly advanced to perpetual profession, until it is certain that he has either satisfied, or been declared perpetually exempt from, the law of active military service.[3]

Active military service includes not only service under arms, but also the "*servizio di sanità*", or hospital duty, which in some localities is given to religious and the clergy, in lieu of

---

[1] *AAS*, III (1911), 37.

[2] S. C. de Rel., Jul. 15, 1919—*AAS*, XI (1919), 321.

[3] *Inter Reliquas*," §1.

actual military drill.[1] Only such active service is to be understood, however, which is prescribed for at least one year.[2] Consequently the prescriptions of the decree will not apply where the military service does not continue for at least an entire year.[3] The decree, moreover, refers only to first service '*Quod ipsi primitus ad militiam vocati*. . ." Consequently any supplementary or extraordinary service to which they may be liable will in no way effect their admission to perpetual profession, once this initial term has been completed.[4]

The decree forbids only admission to perpetual vows, simple or solemn; novices, however, whose time for the service is still somewhat distant, may be admitted to their first profession, after having completed their year of novitiate. They may not, however, make the usual triennial profession now demanded of all religious by canon 574 of the Code, but will make temporal profession extending to the time when they actually enter the service.[5] On the day they actually enter the service, that is, when they *de facto* leave the monastery for the military life,[6] these vows cease to exist; they will also expire if the religious is perpetually declared unfit for the military service.[7] In congregations whose constitutions demand annual profession after the period of probation, novices, obliged to the military service, may make the annual profession and renew this yearly, until called to the service. Once they enter upon their term of service, this annual profession expires;[8] it does not, however, cease if the religious is declared unfit for military life.

---

[1] Fanfani, *De Jure Religiosorum*, p. 277–278; Schaefer, *De Religiosis*, p. 359. Aliter, Vermeersch-Creusen, *Epitome*, I, 429.

[2] Decree "*Inter Reliquas*," §1.

[3] Vermeersch-Creusen, *Epitome*, I, 429; Fanfani, *De Jure Religiosorum*, p. 278.

[4] Vermeersch-Creusen, *loc. cit.*, Fanfani, *loc. cit.*

[5] Decr. "*Inter Reliquas*," §2; S. C. de Rel., 15 Jul. 1919, ad II—*AAS*, XI (1919), 321.

[6] Cf. P. G. R., *CpR*, VII (1926), 104–106.

[7] S. C. de Rel., 15 Jul. 1919—*AAS*, XI (1919), 321. It must be noted that on this point the present legislation differs from the former. According to an interpretation of the decree "*Inter Reliquas*," issued by the Congregation of Religious on February 1, 1912, (*AAS*, IV (1912), 246), temporary vows made before entering the service did not cease with the beginning of the military life.

[8] S. C. de Rel., 30 Nov. 1919—*AAS*, XII (1920), 73.

According to the prescriptions of the Congregation of Religious, issued July 15, 1919, novices obliged to the military service law, will make profession which is to be obligatory until they actually enter the service. A question may arise as to the validity of a profession which, contrary to this prescription, is made for a definite period of time, for three years, for instance, in accordance with canon 574. That it is illicit, is unquestionable. The former decree "*Inter Reliquas*" will shed no light on the question of validity. It declares invalid any perpetual or solemn profession made before the completion of the prescribed term of military service.[1] The response of the Congregation of Religious, of July 15, 1919, prescribing the temporal profession *valitura usque ad servitium militare*, contains no irritating clause, and hence in accordance with canon 11 of the Code, a mild interpretation would be in order, according to which triennial profession, made contrary to the above prescription, would be valid. There seems to be an analogy between the case in question and the prescriptions of canon 574. The latter canon demands that, when the novice has not yet completed his eighteenth year, he will make profession for the entire period of time that must elapse until he reaches the age required for admission to perpetual profession. There is no basis for questioning the validity of his profession, should such a novice make triennial profession at the completion of his novitiate, and then at the expiration of the triennial vows, renew them for the time remaining until he may be validly admitted to perpetual profession. So it seems that the same reasoning could be applied to the question under discussion.[2] In connection with the same case, another question may arise. If contrary to the prescriptions of the Congregation of Religious, triennial vows are made, will they cease if the religious is called to service before the three years have elapsed? According to the decree "*Inter Reliquas*," the answer to this question would be negative, since, as already stated, an interpretation of this decree, made by the Congregation of Religious, on February 1, 1912, declared that temporal vows do not *ipso facto* cease when the religious enters upon his term of service.[3] Moreover, the response of the

---

[1] Cf. "Declarationes Decreti '*Inter Reliquas*'," ad I—*AAS*, IV (1912), 246.

[2] Cf. Larroana, *CpR*, V (1924), 220–222.

[3] Declarationes Decreti "*Inter Reliquas*," ad II.

same Congregation, issued on July 15, 1919, stating that profession ceases to be obligatory with entrance into service, makes use of the word *prædicta*, which may be referred only to the *vota ...valitura usque ad servitium militare*, mentioned in an earlier part of the response. But in accordance with a subsequent response of the Congregation, it is possible to conclude that profession, made for a definite period of time, will also cease when the religious begins his term of military service. In response to a *dubium*, the Congregation, on November 30, 1919,[1] stated that when annual profession is made before entering upon the military life, this annual profession will cease just as soon as the religious is accepted for service and actually enters upon it. This seems to be a manifestation of the mind of the legislator, which intends that all professions, even though made for a definite period of time, should cease with the beginning of the military service.[2]

Although they are freed from their vows during the period of their service, these religious, nevertheless, continue to be members of the community for which they had made temporary vows; they remain subject to the authority and care of the religious superior.[3] If the scene of their military training is near a house of their religious order or institute, these religious must visit it from time to time; but if this is impossible, then they must present themselves betimes for advice and counsel to a priest appointed by the bishop. If no such priest has been appointed, then the religious may select one, and inform the superior of the choice. The Superior General, or his Provincial is moreover bound, either personally, or by means of a delegate, to inquire into the life and conduct of these religious during the time they are absent from the community, in order to take every precaution for the preservation of their faith and vocation.[4]

If during this period of service, the religious decides to quit the religious state and return to the lay state, he is perfectly free to do so. He must, however, inform the superiors of this decision,

---

[1] *AAS*, XII (1920), 73.

[2] This view is held by Maroto, *CpR*, I (1920), 329–330; Larraona, *CpR*, V (1924), 224–225; Schaefer, *De Religiosis*, p. 362.

[3] S. C. de Rel., 15 Jul. 1919—*AAS*, XI (1919), 321.

[4] Decr. "*Inter Reliquas*," §§IV, V.

either in writing, or before witnesses; a record of this declaration must be preserved in the archives of the monastery.[1] But if he decides to persevere in the religious state, he must return to his monastery just as soon as the term of service has been completed. After having spent a few days in spiritual retreat, he must renew his temporal profession for at least one complete year. If before entering upon his military service, the religious had not yet completed three years in temporal profession as required by canon 574, the temporary vows, after his return, must be made for the period yet needed to complete the three interrupted years of temporal profession; but under no circumstances may these temporary vows extend over less than one complete year. Only after all these conditions have been fully complied with, may the religious be validly admitted to make his perpetual profession.[2]

---

[1] S. C. de Rel., 15 Jul. 1919.

[2] Decr. "*Inter Reliquas,*" §VI; declar. Decreti "*Inter Reliquas,*" 1 Feb. 1912, ad VI.

APPENDIX II

DEATHBED PROFESSION OF NOVICES

In his constitution "*Summi Sacerdotis*," of August 23, 1570,[1] Pius V granted to the nuns of the Order of St. Dominic a privilege in virtue of which novices of the order, at the point of death, could be permitted to make profession before the completion of the novitiate, and thereby partake of all the indulgences and other spiritual privileges of the professed religious.[2] In the course of the centuries this privilege was extended to various other religious orders by means of the communication of privileges.[3] Pius X, in a decree "*Spirituali Consolationi*," issued through the Sacred Congregation of Religious, on September 10, 1912, further extended the privilege to all religious orders, congregations, and societies.[4] Because the Code makes no mention of this privilege whatsoever, in the canons bearing on the novitiate or the profession, authorities began to doubt its existence, after the promulgation of the Code. Among the arguments advanced against its existence was the fact that canon 567 §1, by law, grants to all novices a participation in the spiritual favors of the professed, and moreover declares that they have a right to the same suffrages as the professed, should they be overtaken by death, before they are admitted to make their first profession.[5] Other canonists defended the existence of the privilege, on the ground

---

[1] *Bull. Rom.*, IV, pars. 3, p. 123.

[2] "...ita tamen, quod ipsæ moniales novitiæ sic decendentes, indulgentiam et alias gratias, quæ moniales veræ professæ consequuntur, consequi possint." —Const. "*Summi Sacerdotis*," §2.

[3] Piat, *Prælectiones Juris Regularis*, I, 96; Schmalzgrueber, *Jus Ecclesiasticum Universum*, tom. III, pars. IV, tit. XXXI, n. 48; Reiffenstuel, *Jus Canonicum Universum*, tom. III, lib. III, tit. XXXI, n. 182; *et al.*

[4] *AAS*, IV (1912), 589–590.

[5] "Novitii privilegiis omnibus ac spiritualibus gratiis religioni consessis gaudent; et si morte præveniantur, ad eadem suffragia jus habent, quæ proprofessis præscripta sunt."—Can. 567 §1.

that it had been expressly revoked by the canons of the Code.[1] All doubts on this question were dispelled by the response of the Sacred Congregation of Religious, issued on December 30, 1923, in which response the Congregation stated that the privilege had not been recalled, and that it still existed.[2]

The favors granted by the decree "*Spirituali Consolationi*" were the following: 1) participation in all the indulgences, suffrages and graces which could be gained by the professed religious; and 2) a plenary indulgence *in forma jubilæi*. In order to make use of the privilege validly, the decree demanded the fulfillment of the following conditions: 1) it was demanded that the novice had canonically entered upon his year of probaion; 2) the superior who could admit the novice to this profession was the one who was actually in charge of the novitiate house; 3) it was finally required that the usual formula of profession prescribed by the constitution for the regular profession be used, without, however, making any reference to the nature, or duration of the vows.[3] With but one exception, these favors and conditions obtain also now. The exception made by the Congregation of Religious, when it declared that the privilege was still in existence, has reference to the superior for admitting the novice to make the profession. In the decree "*Spirituali Consolationi*," only the superior who was actually in charge of the novitiate house was thus empowered. According to the response of the Congregation of Religious, on the other hand, this power was extended also to the major superiors of the respective institutes.

Besides the spiritual favors granted to this deathbed profession, no other effects follow from it. Should, therefore, the novice die intestate, his property does not pass over to the re-

---

[1] For a complete argumentation of both sides of this question, see Hofmeister, "Professio Religiosa in Articulo Mortis unter dem neuem Recht." —*LQS*, 74 (1921), 493–500, who defends the non-existence. The following canonists argued for the existence of the privilege: Goyeneche, *CpR*, I (1920), 51–52; Schaefer, *Das Ordensrecht*, p. 193; Doink, "Hat das Privileg der Professio Religiosa in articulo mortis nach dem Erscheinen des Codex seine Geltung verloren?"—*LQS*, 75 (1922), 275-278; Raus, "La profession des novices mourants."—*NTR*, 49 (1922), 468–476; *et al.*

[2] S. C. de Rel., "De Professione religiosa in articulo mortis novitiis vel postulantibus permissa."—*AAS*, XV (1923), 156.

[3] Cf. Micheletti, *Jus Pianum*, p. 653.

ligious institute, but reverts to his heirs, according to the prescriptions of the civil law. If, however, the novice recovers, he must first complete his year of probation, and then make a new profession; he is also free to leave the monastery, should he choose not to remain in religious life. At the same time, the religious community may refuse him admission to profession, if he is found to be unsuited for the life of a religious.[1]

In declaring the privilege to be still in existence the Congregation of Religious, in its response, made use of the expression *De novitiis vel postulantibus*. Does this include only novices, or may the privilege be granted also to dying postulants? The response in question refers directly to the former decree "*Spirituali Consolationi*," in which no mention of postulants is made. Hence at first sight one would be inclined to conclude that this response, like the former decree, grants the privilege only to novices. Goyeneche, however, declares that it has since been ascertained that it is the mind of the legislator to extend the decree so as to include also the postulants.[2]

---

[1] Decr. "*Spirituali Consolationi*,"—*AAS*, IV (1912), 589–590; Resp. S. C. de Rel.—*AAS*, XV (1923), 156.

[2] *CpR*, V (1924), 166–167.

BIBLIOGRAPHY

1. Sources

Acta Apostolicæ Sedis, Rome, 1909—

Acta Sanctæ Sedis, 41 vols., Rome, 1865-1908.

Acta et Decreta Sacrorum Conciliorum recentiorum; Collectio Lacensis, 7 vols., Friburgi, Brisgoviæ, 1870-1890.

Bullarium de Sacra Congregatione de Propaganda Fide, 5 vols., Rome, 1839-1841.

Bullarium Diplomatum et Privilegiorum Sanctorum Pontificum Taurinensis edito, auspicante Cardinali Francisco Gaude, 24 vols., Augustæ Taurinorum, 1857–1872.

Canones et Decreta Sacrosancti Oecomenici Tridentini, Editio Novissima ad Fidem Optimorum Exemplarium castigatæ Impressa, 19 ed., Taurini, 1913.

Codex Juris Canonici Pii X Pontificis Maximi jussu digestus Benedicti Papæ XV auctoritate promulgatus, Romæ, 1917.

Codex Theodosianus, ed. P. Krueger, Th. Mommsen, P. M. Meyer, 3 vols., Berolini, 1905.

Codicis Juris Canonici Fontes, cura Emi Petri Card. Gasparri editi, 5 vols., Romæ, 1923–1930.

Corpus Juris Canonici, Editio Lipsiensis II (Richter-Friedberg), 2 vols., Lipsiæ, 1922.

Corpus Juris Civilis, 3 vols., Berolini, 1928–1929.

Decreta Authentica Congregationis Sacrorum Rituum ex actis ejusdem collecta ejusque auctoritate promulgata sub auspiciis SS.D.N. Leonis XIII, 6 vols., Rome, 1898–1912.

Mansi, Joannes Dominicus, *Sacrorum Conciliorum Nova et Amplissima Collectio, 53* vols., Paris, 1901–1919.

Regula S. Basilii Fusius Tractata, (Migne P. G., XXXI, 389 sqq.)

Regula S. Basilii, Brevius Tractata (Migne P. G., XXXI, 1037 sqq.)

Regula S.P.N. Benedicti, Typis Archiabbatiæ S. Vincentii, 1909.

Regula ad Monachos (Cæsarius of Arles) (Migne, P. L., LXVII, 1099 sqq.)

2. Works of Reference

Allies, Thomas W., *The Monastic Life From the Fathers of the Desert to Charlemagne*, London, 1898.

Augustine, Charles, O.S.B., *A Commentary on the New Code of Canon Law*, 8 vols., St. Louis, 1921–1925.

Aryinhac, H. A., SS., *General Legislation in the New Code of Canon Law*, New York, 1930.

Bachofen, P. Charles, O.S.B., *Compendium Juris Regularium*, New York, 1903.

Bakalarczyk, Richard, M.I.C., *De Novitiatu*, Washington, 1927.

Berierle, Ursmer, *L'Orde Monastique des Origines au XIIIe Siecle*, Abbey of Maredsous, 1912.

Besse, J. M., *Les Moines d'Orient Anterieurs au Concile de Chalcedoine*, Paris, 1900.

Biederlack, Josephus, S.J., *De Religiosis Codicis Juris Canonici libri II pars II*, (Can. 487–681)...*denuo recognovit Maximilianus Führich, S.J.*, Oeniponte, 1919.

Billuart, F. Carolus Renatus, *Cursus Theologiæ juxta Mentem Divi Thomæ*, 10 vols., Romæ, 1885.

Bizzarri, Andreas, *Collectanea in usum Secretariæ Sacræ Congregationis Episcoporum et Regularium edita*, Romæ, 1885.

Blat, Albertus, O.P., *Commentarium Textus Codicis Juris Canonici*, 6 vols., Romæ, 1921–1927.

Bouix, D., *Tractatus de Jure Regularium*, 2 vols., 2nd ed., Paris, 1882.

Brandys, Maximilian, O.F.M., *Kirchliches Rechtsbuch für die Religiösen Laiengenossenschaften der Brüder und Schwestern, nach dem neuen Gesetzbuch der hl. Kirche*, 2ed., Paderborn, 1920.

Cance, Adrien, *Le Code de Droit Canonique Commentaire succinct et practique*, 3 vols., Paris, 1928.

Cappello, Felix, M., S.J., *Tractatus Canonico-moralis De Censuris juxta Codicem Juris Canonici*, 2ed., Taurini, 1925.

Cappello, Felix M., S.J., *Summa Juris Canonici, in usum Scholarum Concinnatum*, 2 vols., Romæ, 1928–1930.

Catholic Encyclopedia, 15 vols., New York, 1907–1912.

Chapman, Dom John, O.S.B., *St. Benedict and the Sixth Century*, London, 1929.

Chelodi, Joannes, *Jus Matrimoniale*, 3ed., Tridenti, 1921.

Chelodi, Joannes, *Jus de Personis*, 2ed., Tridenti, 1927.

Chelodi, Joannes, *Jus Pœnale*, Tridenti, 1925.

Cocchi, Guidus, *Commentarium in Codicem Juris Canonici ad Usum Scholarum*, 7 vols., 1925–1927.

De Angelis, Philippus, *Prælectiones Juris Canonici*, 6 vols., Romæ, 1879.

De Meester, A., *Juris Canonici et Juris Canonici-Civilis Compendium*, 3 vols., Brugis, 1921–1928.

Devoti, Joannes, *Institutionum Canonicarum Libri IV*, Leodii, 1883.

Fanfani, Ludovicus, O.P., *De Jure Religiosorum ad Normam Codicis Juris Canonici*, 2ed., Taurini-Romæ, 1925.

Gonzalez, Emmanuel, Tellez, *Commentarium in Decretales Gregorii IX*, 4 vols., Venetiis, 1699.

Grandclaude, E., *Jus Canonicum juxta Ordinem Decretalium*, 3 vols., Paris, 1882.

Hefele, Carl J., *Conciliengeschichte*, 2ed., 9 vols., Freiburg im Br., 1873–1890.

Heimbucher, Max., *Die Orden u. Kongregationen der Katholischen Kirche*, 3 vols., 2ed., Paderborn, 1907–1908.

Herwegen, Ildefons, *Geschichte der Benediktinischen Professformel*, Münster in Westf., 1912.

Humphrey, Wm., S.J., *Elements of Religious Life*, London, 1903.

Hyland, Francis, *Excommunication, its Nature, Historical Development, and Effects*, Washington, 1928.

Jansen, Joseph, O.M.I., *Ordensrecht*, 2ed., Paderborn, 1920.

Kirchenlexikon, 12 vols., 2ed., Freiburg im Breisgau, 1882–1901.

Koch, Hugo, *Virgines Christi, Die Gelübde der Gottgeweihten Jungfrauen in den Ersten Drei Jahrhunderten*, (Texte u. Untersuch. zur Altchristl. Literatur) vol. 31, No. 2, Leipzig, 1907.

Lehmkuhl, Augustinus, S.J., *Casus Conscientiæ*, 2 vols., 4ed., Freiburg, 1913.
Leipoldt, Joannes, *Schenute von Atripe*, (Texte u. Untersuch. zur Altchristl. Literatur, NF. Bd. X, Hft. I), Leipzig, 1903.
Leitner, Martin, *Handbuch des Katholischen Kirchenrechts auf Grund des Neuen Kodex*, 3 vols., 2ed., Regensburg, 1919–1922.
Makee, Ch., *Institutiones Juris Ecclesiastici*, Rome-Paris-Freiburg, 2 vols., 1897.
Maroto, Philippus, *Institutiones Juris Canonici ad Normam Novi Codicis*, 2 vols., 3ed., Romæ, 1921–1923.
Micheletti, A.M., *Jus Pianum*, Taurini, 1914.
Michiels, Gommarus, O.M.Cap., *Normæ Generales Juris Canonici*, 2 vols., Dublin, 1929
Migne, Jacques Paul, *Patrologiæ Cursus Completus—Series Græca*, 161 vols., Paris, 1857–1866.
Migne, Jacques Paul, *Patrologiæ Cursus Completus—Series Latina*, 221 vols., Paris, 1844–1855.
Molitor, Abbas Raphael, O.S.B., *Religiosi Juris Capita Selecta*, Ratisbon, 1909.
Mothon, Joseph, O.P., *Institutions Canoniques a l'uage des Curies Episcopales, du Clerge Paroissial, et de Familles Religieuses*, 2 vols., Paris, 1922.
Munerati, Dantes, SS., *Juris Ecclesiastici Publici et Privati Elementa*, Romæ, 1926.
Murphy, Sr. Margaret Gertrude, *St. Basil and Monasticism*, Washington, 1930.
Noldin, H., S.J., *De Præceptis Dei et Ecclesiæ*, 17ed., Oeniponte, 1924.
Noldin, H., S.J., *De Principiis Theologiæ Moralis*, 17ed., Oeniponte, 1924.
Papi, Hector, S.J., *Religious in Church Law*, New York, 1924.
Papi, Hector, S.J., *Religious Profession, A Commentary on a Chapter of the New Code of Canon Law*, New York, 1918.
Pejska, Joseph, C.SS.R., *Jus Canonicum Religiosorum*, 3ed., Freiburg im Br., 1927.
Petrovits, Joseph, *New Law on Matrimony*, Washington, 1921.
Piatus, F. Montensis, O.F.M., *Prælectiones Juris Regularis*, 2 vols., Tornaci, 1888.
Piontek, Cyrillus, O.F.M., *De Indulto Exclaustrationis necnon Sæcularizationis*, Washington, 1925.
Pirhing, Enricus, S.J., *Jus Canonicum, Novo Methodo Explicatum*, 5 vols., Dilingae, 1674–1678.
Pruemmer, Dominicus, O.P., *Manuale Juris Canonici in Usum Scholarum*, 5ed., Freiburg im Br., 1927.
Raus, J. B., C.SS.R., *De Sacræ Obedientiæ Virtute et Voto, Lugduni*, 1923.
Reiffenstuel, Anacletus, O.F.M., *Jus Canonicum Universum*, 4 vols., Romæ, 1833.
Rodericus, Lustanus, *Quæstiones Regulares*, Lugduni, 1634.
Rothenhæusler, Matthæus, O.S.B., *Zur Aufnahmeordnung der Regula S. Benedicti*, Münster in Westf., 1912.
Sabetti-Barrett, *Compendium Theologiæ Moralis*, 31ed., New York, 1924.
Schaaf, Valentine, O.F.M., *The Cloister*, Washington, 1921.
Schaefer, K. Heinrich, *Die Kanonissenstifter im Deutschen Mittelalter*, Stuttgart, 1907.

Schaefer, Timothy, O.M.Cap., *Das Ordensrecht nach dem Codex Juris Canonici*, Münster, 1923.
Schaefer, Timothy, O.M.Cap., *Compendium De Religiosis ad Normam Codicis Juris Canonici*, Münster in Westf., 1927.
Scharnagl, Anton, *Das Feierliche Gelübde als Ehehinderniss*, Freiburg, 1908.
Schmalzgrueber, Franciscus, S.J., *Jus Ecclesiasticum Universum*, 6 vols., Romæ, 1843–1845.
Sipos, Stephanus, *Enchiridion Juris Canonici*, Pecs, 1926.
Smith, I. Gregory, *Christian Monasticism from the Fourth to the Ninth Century of the Christian Era*, London, 1892.
Suarez, Franciscus, *Opera Omnia*, 26 vols., Paris, 1856–1861.
Thomas, S. Aquinatis, O.P., *Summa Theologica*, 2ed., Romæ, 1894.
Thomassinus, Ludovicus, *Vetus et Nova Ecclesiæ Disciplina*, 3 vols., Venetiis, 1730.
Toso, *Ad Codicem Juris Canonici...Commentaria Minora*, Romæ, 1921—
Turner, Sidney, C.P., *The Vow of Poverty*, Washington, 1929.
Vecchiotti, Septimus, *Institutiones Canonicæ*, 3 vols., 19ed., Augustæ Taurinorum, 1886.
Vermeersch, A., S.J., *De Religiosis Institutis et Personis Tractatus Canonico-moralis*, 2 vols., Brugi, 1909.
Vermeersch, A., S.J., *Theologiæ Moralis Principia-Responsa-Concilia*, 4 vols., Romæ, 1923–1926.
Vermeersch, A.-Creusen, J., *Epitome Juris Canonici cum Commentariis ad Scholas et ad Usum Privatum*, 3 vols., 3ed., Romæ, 1927–1928.
Vicente, Felix, C.M.F., *Recentia Instituta, Opus Canonicum*, Madrid, 1916.
Wernz-Vidal, *Jus Matrimoniale*, 2ed., Romæ, 1928.
Wernz-Vidal, *Jus de Personis*, 2ed., Romæ, 1928.
Woywod, Stanislaus, O.F.M., *A Practical Commentary on the Code of Canon Law*, 2 vols., 3ed., New York, 1929.
Zoeckler, Otto, *Askese und Mönchtum*, Frankfurt a. M., 1897.

3. Periodicals

American Ecclesiastical Review, Philadelphia, 1889—
Analecta Juris Pontificii, Romæ, 1855–1868, Paris, 1869–1890.
Archiv für Katholisches Kirchenrecht, Mainz, 1857—
Commentarium pro Religiosis, Romæ, 1920—
Ephemerides Liturgicæ, Romæ, 1887—
Homiletic and Pastoral Review, New York, 1900—
Irish Ecclesiastical Record, Dublin, 1864—
Nouvelle Revue Theologique, Tournai-Paris, 1869—
Periodica de re canonica et morali utili præsertim Religiosis et Missionariis, Brugis, 1905—
Revue des Communautes Religieuses, Louvain, 1925—
Revue Thomiste, Paris, 1893—
Stimmen aus Maria-Laach, Freiburg im Br., 1871—
Theologisch-praktische Quartalschrift, Linz, 1832—

UNIVERSITATIS CATHOLICA AMERICAE

WASHINGTON, D.C.

FACULTAS IURIS CANONICI

1930—1931

No. 63

Deus Lux Mea

TITULI

Quos

AD DOCTORATUS GRADUM

IN

IURE CANONICO

APUD UNIVERSITATEM CATHOLICAM AMERICÆ

CONSEQUENDUM
PUBLICE PROPUGNABIT

WOLFGANGUS NORBERTUS FREY

Sacerdos Ordinis Sancti Benedicti
Iuris Canonici Licentiatus

HORA XI A.M. DIE XXVI MAJI A.D. MCMXXXI

TITULI

De Jure Canonico

I	De Dissertatione.	
II	De Historia Juris Canonici.	
III	Canones 1–7	De Ambitu Codicis.
IV	Canones 8–24	De Legibus Ecclesiasticis.
V	Canones 25–30	De Consuetudine
VI	Canones 31–35	De Temporis Suppotatione.
VII	Canones 63–79	De Privilegiis
VIII	Canones 80–86	De Dispensationibus
IX	Canones 87–107	Generales Notiones de Personis.
X	Canones 111–117	De Clericorum Adscriptione alicui Dioeecesi.
XI	Canones 118–123	De Juribus et Privilegiis Clericorum.
XII	Canones 124–144	De Obligationibus Clericorum.
XIII	Canones 145–195	De Officiis Ecclesiasticis.
XIV	Canones 196–210	De Postestate Ordinaria et Delegata.
XV	Canones 487–498	De Notione, Erectione, Suppressione Religionis.
XVI	Canones 499–537	De Religionum Regimine.
XVII	Canones 1019–1034	De iis Quæ Matrimonii Celebratione præmitti debent.
XVIII	Canones 1035–1057	De Impedimentis in Genere.
XIX	Canones 1058–1066	De Impedimentis Impedientibus.
XX	Canones 1068–1080	De Impedimentis Dirimentibus.
XXI	Canones 1081–1093	De Consensu Matrimoniali.
XXII	Canones 1094–1103	De Forma Celebrationis Matrimonii.
XXIII	Canones 1104–1107	De Matrimonio Conscientiæ.
XXIV	Canones 1108–1109	De Tempore et Loco Celebrationis Matrimonii.
XXV	Canones 1110–1117	De Matrimonii Effectibus.
XXVI	Canones 1118–1127	De Dissolutione Vinculi.
XXVII	Canones 1552–1556	De Notione Judicii et de Foro Competenti.
XXVIII	Canones 1569–1607	De Variis Tribunalium Gradibus et Speciebus.
XXIX	Canones 1608–1645	De Disciplina in Tribunalibus servanda.
XXX	Canones 1646–1666	De Partibus in Causa.
XXXI	Canones 1667–1705	De Actionibus et Exceptionibus
XXXII	Canones 1706–1725	De Causæ Introductione.
XXXIII	Canones 1726–1746	De Litis Contestatione, de Litis Instantia, et de Interrogationibus Partibus in Judicio Faciendis.

XXXIV	Canones 1747–1836	De Probationibus.
XXXV	Canones 1837–1857	De Causis Incidentibus.
XXXVI	Canones 1865–1877	De Processus Publicatione, de Conclusione in Causa, de Causæ Discussione, et de Sententia.
XXXVII	Canones 2147–2161	De Modo Procedendi in Remotione Parochorum Inamovibilium et Amovibilium.
XXXVIII	Canones 2186–2194	De Suspensione ex Informata Conscientiæ.
XXXIX	Canones 2195–2198	De Natura Delicti ejusque Divisione.
XL	Canones 2199–2211	De Imputabilitate Delicti, de Causis illam aggravantibus, vel minuentibus, et de Juridicia Delicti Effectibus.
XLI	Canones 2212–2213	De Conatu Delicti
XLII	Canones 2214–2240	De Pœnis in Genere.
XLIII	Canones 2241–2285	De Pœnis Medicinalibus seu de Censuris.
XLIV	Canones 2286–2305	De Pœnis Vindicativis.
XLV	Canones 2306–2313	De Remediis Pœnalibus et Pœnitentiis.

De Jure Romano

XLVI	The Periods of Roman Law.
XLVII	Furtum.
XLVIII	Damnum Injuria Datum.
XLIX	Slavery.
L	Citizenship.
LI	Marriage.
LII	Patria Potestas.
LIII	Personæ in Manu.
LIV	Personæ in Mancipio.
LV	Tutela.
LVI	Cura.
LVII	Possessio.
LVIII	Proprietas.
LIX	Adoptio et Adrogatio.
LX	The Roman Family.

Vidit Facultas:

VALENTINUS SCHAAF, O.F.M., J.C.D., *Vice Decanus.*
LUDOVICUS H. MOTRY, S.T.D., J.C.D., *a Secretis.*
FRANCISCUS J. LARDONE, S.T.D., J.U.D.

Vidit Rector Magnificus Universitatis:

JACOBUS HUGO RYAN, PH.D., S.T.D., LL.D., LITT.D.

BIOGRAPHICAL NOTE

Wolfgang Norbert Frey was born in St. Marys, Pa., on the third of April, 1903. After receiving his elementary education in the parochial schools of that city, he entered the Scholasticate department of St. Vincent College, Latrobe, Pa., in the fall of 1915, where he completed his classical course in June, 1922. He was received into the Benedictine Novitiate of St. Vincent Archabbey, in July of the same year. After his profession, on July 11, 1923, he attended the prescribed Seminary courses, and was ordained to the Sacred Priesthood on June 16, 1929. In September of the same year, his Superiors sent him to take up graduate studies in the School of Canon Law of the Catholic University of America.

CATHOLIC UNIVERSITY OF AMERICA

Canon Law Studies

1. Freriks, Rev. Celestine A., C.PP.S., J.C.D., Religious Congregations in Their External Relations, 121 pp., 1916.

2. Galliher, Rev. Daniel M., O.P., J.C.D., Canonical Elections, 117 pp., 1917.

3. Borkowski, Rev. Aurelius L., O.F.M., J.C.D., De Confraternitatibus Ecclesiasticis, 136 pp., 1918.

4. Castillo, Rev. Cayo, J.C.D., Disertacion Historico-canonica sobre la Potestad del Cabildo en Sede Vacante o Impedida del Vicario Capitular, 99 pp., 1919 (1918).

5. Kubelbeck, Rev. William J., S.T.B., J.C.D., The Sacred Penitentiaria and Its Relations to Faculties of Rrdinaries and Priests, 129pp., 1918.

6. Petrovits, Rev. Joseph J. C., S.T.D., J.C.D., The New Church Law on Matrimony, X-461 pp., 1919.

7. Hickey, Rev. John J., S.T.B., J.C.D., Irregularities and Simple Impediments in the New Code of Canon Law, 100 pp., 1920.

8. Klekotka, Rev. Peter J., S.T.B., J.C.D., Diocesan Concultors, 179 pp., 1920.

9. Wannenmacher, Rev. Francis, J.C.D., The Evidence in Ecclesiastical Procedure Affecting the Marriage Bond, 1920. (Not Printed.)

10. Golden, Rev. Henry Francis, J.C.D., Parochial Benefices in the New Code, IV-119 pp., 1921. (Printed 1925).

11. Koudelka, Rev. Charles J., J.C.D., Pastors, Their Rights and Duitues According to the New Code of Canon Law, 211 pp., 1921.

12. Melo, Rev. Antonius, O.F.M., J.C.D., De Exemptione Regularium, X-188 pp., 1921.

13. Schaaf, Rev. Valentine Theodore, O.F.M., S.T.B., J.C.D., The Cloister, X-180 pp., 1921.

14. Burke, Rev. Thomas Joseph, S.T.B., J.C.D., Competence in Ecclesiastical Tribunals, IV-117 pp., 1922.

15. Leech, Rev. George Leo, J.C.D., A Comparative Study of the Constitution "Apostolicæ Sedis" and the "Codex Juris Canonici," 179 pp., 1922.
16. Motry, Rev. Hubert Louis, S.T.D., J.C.D., Diocesan Faculties According to the Code of Canon Law, II-167 pp., 1922.
17. Murphy, Rev. George Lawrence, J.C.D., Delinquencies and Penalties in the Administration and Reception of the Sacraments, IV-121 pp., 1923.
18. O'Reilly, Rev. John Anthony, S.T.B., J.C.D., Ecclesiastical Sepulture in the New Code of Canon Law, II-129 pp., 1923.
19. Michalicka, Rev. Wenceslas Cyrill, O.S.B., J.C.D., Judicial Procedure in Dismissal of Clerical Exe,mpt Religious 107 pp., 1923.
20. Dargin, Rev. Edward Vincent, S.T.B., J.C.D., Reserved Cases According to the Code of Canon Law, IV-103 pp., 1924.
21. Godfrey, Rev. John A., S.T.B., J.C.D., The Right of Patronage According to the Code of Canon Law, 153 pp., 1924.
22. Hagedorn, Rev. Francis Edward. J.C.D., General Legislation on Indulgences, II-154 pp., 1924.
23. King, Rev. James Ignatius, J.C.D., The Administration of the Sacraments to Dying Non-Catholics, V-141 pp., 1924.
24. Winslow, Rev. Francis Joseph, A.F.M., J.C.D., Vicars and Prefects Apostolic, IV-149 pp., 1924.
25. Correa, Rev. Jose Servelion, S.T.L., J.C.D., La Potesdad Legislativa de la Iglesia Catolica, IV-127 pp., 1925.
26. Dugan, Rev. Henry Francis, A.M., J.C.D., The Judiciary Department of the Diocesan Curia, 87 pp., 1925.
27. Keller, Rev. Charles Frederick, S.T.B., J.C.D., Mass Stipends, 167 pp., 1925.
28. Paschang, Rev. John Linus, J.C.D., The Sacramentals According to the Code of Canon Law, 129 pp., 1925.
29. Piontek, Rev. Cyrillus, O.F.M., S.T.B., J.C.D., De Indulto Exclaustrationis necnon Sæcularizationis, XIII-289 pp., 1929.
30. Kearney, Rev. Richard Joseph, S.T.B., J.C.D., Sponsors at Baptism According to the Code of Canon Law, IV-127 pp., 1925.
31. Bartlett, Rev. Chester Joseph, A.M., LL.B., J.C.D., The Tenure of Parochial Property in the United States of America, V-108 pp., 1926.
32. Kilker, Rev. Adrian Jerome, J.C.D., Extreme Unction, V-425 pp., 1926.
33. McCormick, Rev. Robert Emmet, J.C.D., Confessors of Religious, VIII-266 pp., 1926.

34. Miller, Rev. Newton Thomas, J.C.D., Founded Masses According to the Code of Canon Law, VII-93 pp., 1926.

35. Roelker, Eev. Rdward G., S.T.D., J.C.D., Principles of Privilege According to the Code of Canon Law, XI-166 pp., 1926.

36. Bakalarczyk, Rev. Richardus, M.I.C., J.U.D., De Novitiatu, VIII-208 pp., 1927.

37. Pizzuti, Rev. Lawrence, O.F.M., J.U.L., De Parochis Religiosis, 1929.

38. Bliley, Rev. Nicholas Martin, O.S.B., J.C.D., Altars According to the Code of Canon Law, XIX-132 pp., 1927.

39. Brown, Brendan Francis, A.B., LL.M., J.U.D., The Canonical Juristic Personality with Special Reference to is Status in the United States of America, V-212 pp., 1927.

40. Cavanaugh, Rev. William Thomas, C.P., J.U.D., The Reservation of the Blessed Sacrament, VIII-101 pp., 1927.

41. Doheny, Rev. William J., C.S.C., A.B., J.U.D., Church Property; Modes of Acquisition, X-118 pp., 1927.

42. Feldhaus, Rev. Aloysius H., C.PP.S., J.C.D., Oratories, IX-141 pp., 1927.

43. Kelly, Rev. James Patrick, A.B., J.C.D., The Jurisdiction of the Simple Confessor, X-208 pp., 1927.

44. Neuberger, Rev. Nicholas J., J.C.D., Canon 6, or the Relation of the Codex Juris Canonici to the Preceding Legislation, V-95 pp., 1927.

45. O'Keeffe, Rev. Gerald Michael, J.C.D., Matrimonial Dispensations, Powers of Bishops, Priests, and Confessors, VIII-232 pp., 1927.

46. Quigley, Rev. Joseph, A.M., A.B., J.C.D., Condemned Societies, 139 pp., 1927.

47. Zaplotnik, Rev. Ioannes Leo, J.C.D., De Vicariis Foraneis, X-142, 1927.

48. Duskie, Rev. John Aloysius, A.B., J.C.D., The Canonical Status of the Orientals in the United States, VIII-196 pp., 1928.

49. Hyland, Rev. Francis Edward, J.C.D., Excommunication, Its Nature, Historical Development and Effects, VIII-181 pp., 1928.

50. Reinmann, Rev. Gerald Joseph, O.M.C., J.C.D., The Third Order Secular of Saint Francis, 201 pp., 1928.

51. Schenk, Rev. Francis J., J.C.D., The Matrimonial Impediments of Mixed Religion and Disparity of Cult, XVI-318 pp., 1929.

52. Coady, Rev. John Joseph, S.T.D., J.U.D., A.M., The Appointment of Pastors, VIII-150 pp., 1929.

53. Kay, Rev. Thomas Henry, J.C.D., Competence in Matrimonial Procedure, VIII-164 pp., 1929.

54. Turner, Rev. Sidney Joseph, C.P., J.U.D., The Vow of Poverty, XLIX-217 pp., 1929.

55. Kearney, Rev. Raymond A., A.B., S.T.D., J.C.D., The Principles of Delegation, VII-149 pp., 1929.

56. Conran, Rev. Edward James, A.B., J.C.D., The Interdict, V-163 pp., 1930.

57. O'Neill, Rev. William H., J.C.D., Papal Rescripts of Favor, VII-218 pp., 1930.

58. Bastnagel, Rev. Clement Vincent, J.U.D., The Appointment of Parochial Adjutants and Assistants, XV-257 pp., 1930.

59. Ferry, Rev. William A., A.B., J.C.D., Stole Fees, X-107 pp., 1930.

60. Costello, Rev. John Michael, A.B., J.C.D., Domicile and Quasi-Domicile, VII-201 pp., 1930.

61. Kremer, Rev. Michael Nicholas, A.B., S.T.B., J.C.D., Church Support in the United States, VI-136 pp., 1930.

62. Angulo, Rev. Luis Martinez, C.M., J.C.L., Legislacion de la Iglesia Catholica sobre la intencion en la aplicacion de la Misa, 1931.

63. Frey, Rev. Wolfgang Norbert, O.S.B., A.B., J.C.L., The Act of Religious Profession, 1931.

64. Roberts, Rev. James Brendan, A.B., J.C.L., The Banns of Matrimony, 1931.

65. Ryder, Rev. Raymond Aloysius, A.B., J.C.L., Simony, 1931.

66. Campagna, Michael Angelo, Ph.B., J.U.L., Il Vacario Generale del Vescovo, 1931.

67. Cox, Rev. Joseph Godfrey, A.B., J.C.L., The Administration of Seminaries, 1931.

68. Gregory, Rev. Donald Joseph, S.T.B., J.U.L., The Pauline Privilege, 1931.

69. Donohue, Rev. John Francis, M.A., J.C.L., The Impediment of Crime, 1931.

70. Dooley, Rev. Eugene Aloysius, O.M.I., J.C.L., Church Law on Sacred Relics, 1931.

THE ARCHABBEY PRESS
LATROBE, PENNSYLVANIA

PRINTED IN THE U.S.A.

www.ingramcontent.com/pod-product-compliance
Lightning Source LLC
LaVergne TN
LVHW050232080826
844660LV00012B/518

* 9 7 8 0 8 1 3 2 2 2 5 2 3 *